Making Sense of Education Policy

For Natalie

Making Sense of Education Policy

Studies in the Sociology and Politics of Education

GEOFF WHITTY

Director, Institute of Education, University of London

P·C·P

Paul Chapman
Publishing

Paul Chapman Publishing
A SAGE Publications Company
6 Bonhill Street
London EC2A 4PU

SAGE Publications Inc
2455 Teller Road
Thousand Oaks, California 91320

SAGE Publictions India Pvt Ltd
32, M-Block Market
Greater Kailash – I
New Delhi 1 10 048

British Library Cataloguing in Publication Data

A catalogue record for this book is available from the British Library

ISBN 0 7619 7451 2
ISBN 0 7619 7452 0 (pbk)
Library of Congress catalogue record available

October 28, 2003

Typeset by PDQ Typesetting, Newcastle-under-Lyme
Printed and bound in Great Britain by Athenaeum Press, Gateshead

Contents

Acknowledgements

Chapter 1 is based upon the Karl Mannheim Memorial Lecture, which I delivered at the Institute of Education, University of London, in January 1997 on the fiftieth anniversary of Mannheim's death. Chapter 2 was originally given as a lecture at the Second International Conference of the Sociology of Education in Portugal at the University of the Algarve, Faro, Portugal, in September 1993. Chapter 3 is based on lectures given at the Havens Center, University of Wisconsin-Madison, USA in November 1996, updated for a presentation to an international symposium on 'Futures of Education' in Zurich, Switzerland in March 2000. Chapter 4 is based on a talk given at the Annual Conference of the Standing Committee for the Education and Training of Teachers in Rugby in November 1999. Chapter 5 is based on a lecture given at the National Taiwan Normal University in March 1995, while Chapter 6 was presented at the World Congress of Comparative Education Societies in Sydney, Australia in July 1996. Most of Chapter 7 was a lecture given at a Catholic Education Service conference on 'Catholic Schools in Urban Poverty Areas' at Swanwick, Derbyshire in July 1999 with some additional material from a paper presented at a seminar on 'Education Policy and Social Class' at King's College London in July 2000. Chapter 8 was originally delivered as a lecture at the University of Oxford in February 1998, but has been updated with material drawn from a talk to the Headstrong Club in Lewes in May 2001.

Chapter 2 was co-authored by Peter Aggleton and Gabrielle Rowe (now Ivinson), and Chapters 3 and 6 were written with Sally Power, so I am most grateful for their permission to include these papers in this volume. I am also grateful to Peter Mortimore for allowing me to use those parts of Chapter 7 that are based on a pamphlet we wrote together in 1997. Some of the other chapters also draw heavily on work carried out with colleagues, notably Peter Aggleton, Michael Apple, Elizabeth Barrett, Len Barton, David Crook, Marny Dickson, Tony Edwards, John Furlong, Eva Gamarnikow, Sharon Gewirtz, David Halpin, Sheila Miles, Sally Power, Paul Tyrer, Caroline Whiting and Deborah Youdell. However, while my own understanding of the issues has benefited enormously from these collaborations, the responsibility for the particular formulations published here rests entirely with me.

The Economic and Social Research Council provided support for some of the research upon which the book is based. I am also indebted to the University of Wisconsin-Madison, USA and the University of Canterbury, Christchurch, New Zealand, for visiting fellowships which enabled me to undertake research and work on some of the lectures that now form the chapters of this book.

I would like to thank Marcia Beer for her help in preparing the manuscript.

1

Introduction: Sociology and Education Policy

This introductory chapter locates the sociological study of education policy within a tradition that goes back to the distinguished European sociologist Karl Mannheim. Although better known for his work on social theory and the sociology of knowledge, Mannheim became increasingly concerned with the sociology of education and education policy when working at the London School of Economics and the Institute of Education in the 1940s. I argue here that, although the particular approach adopted by Mannheim may be inappropriate today, many of the questions he asked remain relevant and his use of sociological concepts to help make sense of education policy sets an important example for contemporary sociologists of education to follow.

This book reflects my own struggle to make sense of changes in education policy over the past ten years, using the resources of the sociology and politics of education. In some ways, it is a sequel to my earlier book, *Sociology and School Knowledge: Curriculum Theory, Research and Politics* (Whitty, 1985), which used similar disciplinary resources to explore changes in the school curriculum. The present volume brings together and updates a series of lectures given during the past decade. It represents my developing understanding not only of education policies at the turn of the millennium but also of the conceptual tools that have proved helpful for understanding those policies in my own research and teaching.

Ten years ago, in 1992, I moved within the University of London from the Goldsmiths Chair of Policy and Management in Education at Goldsmiths College to the Karl Mannheim Chair of Sociology of Education at the Institute of Education. The latter chair, previously held by Basil Bernstein, was named after the eminent Hungarian sociologist, Karl Mannheim, who worked at the Institute in the 1940s. During the eight years that I held that chair,[1] I sought to build on the strong tradition of sociology of education as a discipline at the Institute, but particularly sought to utilise it to explore the sorts of issues in policy and management that I had tried to grapple with in my previous post. The different ways in which I have tried to do this are reflected in the selection of work presented here. Some of the chapters draw on findings from empirical

1

research, while others are more theoretical or speculative in nature. Although much of the substantive content relates to education policy in England and Wales, I have also included some material based on comparative studies of education policy.

In this chapter, I consider the extent to which the tradition of sociological work that began at the Institute with Karl Mannheim still has relevance to the study of education policy today.[2] Mannheim was born into a middle-class Jewish family in Hungary at the end of the nineteenth century. He gained his Doctorate in philosophy in 1918 at the University of Budapest, after studying in Berlin, Paris, Freiburg and Heidelberg as well as Budapest itself. Significantly for his later career, he mixed freely in both positivist and anti-positivist circles. Nevertheless, he became most closely associated with the group that had gathered around George Lukács, the Marxist literary critic who was briefly a Commissioner for Education in a short-lived Communist–Social Democratic coalition government. Although Mannheim declined to join the Communist Party, Lukács appointed him as a lecturer at the College of Education of the University of Budapest, which he later described in his curriculum vitae of August 1945 as Hungary's nearest equivalent to the Institute of Education in London.

As a result of his association with Lukács, Mannheim fell foul of the new counter-revolutionary government in Budapest and left for Vienna in December 1919. From there, he moved to Germany and many of his most formative intellectual experiences took place in exile in Weimar Germany. He went initially to Freiburg and Berlin but settled in Heidelberg, where he was a member of the circle that had grown up around Max Weber and had continued to meet (under Alfred Weber) after his death in 1920. In 1930, Mannheim became Professor of Sociology and head of a newly created College of Sociology at the Goethe University of Frankfurt. In 1933, he was 'retired' by the Nazis from his position in Frankfurt and came, via Amsterdam, to England where he held a temporary lectureship in sociology at the London School of Economics (LSE).

The distinguished educationist, Sir Fred Clarke, who was the Director of the Institute of Education at that time, had been impressed by his contact with Mannheim at meetings of the Moot, a group of intellectuals that included such notables as J. H. Oldham, Adolph Lowe, J. Middleton Murry, Sir Walter Moberly, Lord A. D. Lindsay and T. S. Eliot. In 1941 Clarke therefore arranged for Mannheim to teach classes at the Institute on a part-time basis while he was still working at the LSE. Negotiating this arrangement with the LSE was not straightforward, because of the strained relations between Mannheim and the Professor of Sociology, Morris Ginsberg, and it was only secured because of the close friendship between Clarke and the then Director of the LSE, Professor A. M. Carr-Saunders (Kettler et al., 1984; Woldring, 1986). For two years, it involved Mannheim travelling between his home in Hampstead to Nottingham, where the Institute was evacuated for much of the war, and Cambridge, where the LSE was based during the war.

As early as March 1943, Clarke was arguing the case for appointing someone like Mannheim – and he clearly had Mannheim himself in mind – to a new professorial position at the Institute as soon as the war was over. In a note to the Delegacy responsible for the Institute, he wrote:

> The case for a professorship to work in terms of the sociological approach may be related to the uneasy awareness, now so widespread and yet so ill-defined, that great changes in the social order and the inter-play of social forces are already in progress – and that educational theory and educational policy that take no account of these will be not only blind but positively harmful.
>
> (Sir Fred Clarke, Director, Institute of Education, 18 March 1943)

In the event, on 1 January 1946, Mannheim succeeded to Clarke's own chair in education, which on Clarke's retirement became separated from the Directorship of the Institute on the grounds that, while his successors as Director 'might well continue to carry the title and status of Professor [it was] too much to expect them to go on functioning in that capacity to any degree of effectiveness'. Although Mannheim's chair was in education, he took special responsibility for the sociological aspects of the field. His own conception of his post was a broad one influenced by his background and interests in philosophy, sociology and social psychology. He also approached it in much the same spirit as the International Library of Sociology and Social Reconstruction, which he founded and which reflected his conviction that sociology could provide the basis for a postwar social reconstruction in which education would play a vital role.

Mannheim held his chair at the Institute of Education for little more than one year before his untimely death at the age of 53 on 9 January 1947. My own life overlapped with Mannheim's by little over a week. This can hardly entitle me to claim membership of the same generation let alone the same 'generation unit' – to cite one of his concepts that has survived into the contemporary literature. Yet, I believe that, even though there have been major changes in the past fifty years, there are some striking continuities which suggest that parts of the legacy of Karl Mannheim are well worth holding onto. I hope they are apparent in the examples of my own writing contained in this book.

Mannheim for today?

Certainly, the argument for having sociologists involved in the study of education is at least as strong as it was when Clarke was arguing the case fifty years ago. There is a similar widespread sense today that significant but ill-defined changes in the nature of the social order are in progress. Not only sociologists, but also the 'quality' media, constantly debate the implications of living in postmodernity, a post-industrial society, late capitalism, high modernity, a post-traditional society or whatever they choose to call it. Chris Shilling, one of the most insightful of today's sociologists of education in Britain, who favours the concept of 'high modernity', has written:

> Modernity brought with it a period of rapid change and the promise of control. In contrast, high modernity is a 'runaway world' which is apparently out of control...The consequences of high modernity... have the effect of introducing a radical doubt as to what precise goals education should achieve. These consequences also throw into question whether education systems have the capacity either to be fully controlled, or to accomplish planned social change with any degree of accuracy.
>
> (Shilling, 1993: 108)

I want to suggest that, long before modernity was thought to have run its course, Mannheim was struggling with similar issues even though he responded to them in rather different terms. He once wrote that he wanted to learn 'the secret (even if it is infernal) of these new times', confronting problems that Kettler and Meja (1995) suggest, in the introduction to one of their books on Mannheim, should remain 'irresistible to reflective people at the end of the twentieth century' (1995: 1). Yet Mannheim barely gets a mention in the voluminous works of Shilling's mentor, Anthony Giddens, generally regarded as Britain's leading contemporary social theorist and current Director of the London School of Economics.

Although Mannheim's work on the sociology of knowledge is still cited in other contemporary literature, as is his work on generation, Denis Lawton (1975) has quite rightly pointed to his relative neglect in education studies, even in the 1970s when his work on the social determination of ideas might have been expected to commend itself to the then 'new' sociologists of education. With only a few exceptions (e.g. Lander, 1983), his work has not in recent years been seen as a major theoretical resource for research even in the sociology of education at the Institute and elsewhere in Britain. Indeed, even what is generally regarded as his most important work, *Ideology and Utopia* (Mannheim, 1936), has been borrowed from the Institute of Education library only a handful of times since the early 1970s.

In some ways, of course, this neglect is justified. It would, after all, be easy to exaggerate the extent to which Mannheim is a contemporary thinker. Not only would this be in some tension with the thrust of his own writings on the sociology of knowledge, it would involve doing a considerable degree of violence to his texts. To give but one example, I read with interest in an intellectual biography of Mannheim that he had written about the prevalence of 'an attitude of believing in nothing' and 'an endless craving for new sensations' (Loader, 1985: 189), statements that resonate with some contemporary characterisations of postmodernity. Yet when I traced this back to its source in *Diagnosis of Our Time* (Mannheim, 1943), I read:

> Whereas in some prominent individuals...falling into the abyss of the self without reaching the bottom presents itself as a grandiose struggle, a new Titanism, in the average man the very same dynamics lead to a frivolous attitude of believing in nothing and an endless craving for new sensations.
>
> (p. 108)

In both style and content, this sentiment places Mannheim in a very different age from our own, though even one of his own contemporaries, Professor Cavanagh of King's College, suggested that, perhaps because 'the German way of writing doesn't fit English', Mannheim's writings seemed 'to say little in a large number of obscure words' (Cavanagh to Clarke, 10 September 1942). Furthermore, the character of his work does not always make it easy for us to be clear what Mannheim is saying. Although one of his posthumous volumes was entitled *Systematic Sociology* (Mannheim, 1957), Mannheim was hardly a systematic thinker. His work may be charitably considered what his intellectual biographer, Colin Loader (1985), euphemistically terms a 'dynamic totality', but even the books compiled during his lifetime under his own supervision are full of inconsistencies and repetitions.

Yet, I still believe his work as a whole deserves considerably more attention than it has recently received. As Meja and Kettler (1993) put it: 'Mannheim confronts many contemporary sociologists with their hopes and misgivings, and offers them a model for resourceful thinking' (1993: xxxiv). Even some of the themes he addressed are surprisingly contemporary or at least relate to issues that continue to concern us, both in sociology and in education. His more theoretical work on the sociology of knowledge was unfashionable among Marxist sociologists of education in the 1970s partly because he resisted the notion that all ideas could be understood in terms of relations of class. But, notwithstanding the unremitting maleness of his language, one might have expected him to be cited more by feminist writers in the 1980s, as unusually among male sociologists of his era (and some would say since) he had pointed out that women's interests were not best served by constantly having their voices mediated by men (Meja and Kettler, 1993: xxxii). And, in so far as he generalised this argument to all social groups, it might be thought surprising that his work has not been recuperated in the 1980s and 1990s by contemporary writers who question the primacy not only of class relations, but even that of the 'holy trinity' of class, race and gender. Furthermore, his discussion of the growth of 'social techniques' which penetrate deep into our private lives and subject 'to public control psychological processes which were formerly considered as purely personal' in some ways anticipates Foucault's concern with 'moral technologies'. Finally, some of his discussions of consciousness and awareness anticipate contemporary notions of reflexivity.

Even so, it would be extremely difficult to characterise Mannheim as a post-structuralist or postmodernist theorist by any stretch of the imagination. His social psychology of personality was at odds with the notion of the decentred subject and the various 'solutions' he sought and provided to the 'problem' of relativism retain little currency today. His work was also firmly set in the redemptive project of the Enlightenment, albeit in the light of a recognition that it was in danger of all going horribly wrong. Thus, not only did his roots predispose him towards a 'grand narrative' approach to theory, his own solutions to a 'runaway world' were classicly modernist ones. Kettler and Meja (1995) suggest that his 'project was to link thinking to emancipation – despite strong evidence against the connection' (1995: 1)!

Nevertheless, like Mannheim, many contemporary sociologists still struggle with the prospect of losing any basis for claiming the superiority of one account over another – and continue to seek a viable epistemological basis for social science and social intervention. To put the problem in contemporary sociological jargon, rather than that of his own times, Mannheim sought a way of rejecting essentialism and foundationalism without being disempowered in the process. This has remained a recurring theme within social theory and in the sociology of education. Not only is it a major concern for those writers who still seek a basis for action in an uncertain world in the light of postmodernist critiques of social science, it is also the very issue that the 'new sociologists of education' at the Institute (Young, 1971) struggled with in the early 1970s and which Michael Young sought for a time to address through the social phenomenology of Merleau Ponty (Young, 1973).

Subsequently, that particular Latin turn in the sociology of education was swiftly overshadowed by an Althusserian one and more recently by a Foucauldian one. However, other sociologists of education eschewed that theoretical response to the cold climate facing them under Thatcherism in the 1980s in favour of a move into policy studies. For example, Brian Davies says of me, in his own inimitable way, that I have 'moved with some decorum, rather than any hint of "scramble", from being "new directions" first insider-critic to neo-Marxist curriculum analyst..., to policy researcher and theorist' (Davies, 1994: 14). In some ways, that move too was prefigured in Mannheim's own career. Jean Floud, who knew Mannheim in the 1930s and was later Reader in the Sociology of Education at the Institute of Education, suggests that by the 1940s Mannheim 'had turned from the fine points of the diagnosis [of the crisis] to the active political problem of controlling the descent into disaster' (Floud, 1959: 49). Put another way, the detached critical observer had 'grown into the political and social strategist who tries to understand so that others may be able to act' (Bramstedt and Gerth, 1951: xii). And, in proposing 'Planning for Freedom' – a Third Way between a laissez-faire society and total regimentation (Mannheim, 1951: xvii) – Mannheim went even further to suggest how they should act. With the hindsight of the late 1950s, Floud wrote dismissively of Mannheim's 'joyful conviction that Sociology, the science of social action, can banish or mitigate the horrors of social change' (Floud, 1959: 42). Although Mannheim's obituary in *The Times* claimed that he himself always insisted that he was concerned with diagnosis only, Campbell Stewart has suggested that his denial of partisanship was 'rather like Mr Roosevelt's claim to be neutral before Pearl Harbor' (Stewart, 1967).

According to Yoshiyuki Kudomi, a Mannheimian scholar from Japan, Mannheim certainly did not abandon the one project for the other (Kudomi, 1996). Whether or not he actually made significant contributions to social theory after the mid-1930s, he continued to argue the need for sociological analysis alongside what he called 'social education' or the development of the techniques necessary for the creation of the democratic personality. He always regarded his prescriptions for policy in 'Planning for Freedom' as informed by his social theory even if that was not always clear to others.

Part of the reason why Floud and others could regard Mannheim's quest as irrelevant in the 1950s and beyond was that his diagnosis did not seem directly applicable to postwar social democracy. However, it is at least arguable that, after the experience of deregulation and political hostility to planning under Margaret Thatcher and her successors in Britain and elsewhere, Mannheim's ideas about the damaging effects of atomisation and a laissez-faire society now have considerably more pertinence than they did then. In an interview with Kudomi in 1991, Campbell Stewart – a student of Mannheim, who later developed his writings on the sociology of education into a textbook (Mannheim and Stewart, 1962) – mused about what Mannheim's reaction might have been to Mrs Thatcher's notion that 'there is no such thing as society' (*Woman's Own*, 31 October 1987). Similarly, Madeleine Arnot (1998) has suggested that it is salutory to re-read Mannheim in the current context of 'heightened individualism and atomism in society'. There is certainly some poetic justice in Mannheim's ideas becoming relevant at the end of the Thatcherite era, since his views were one of the main targets of Frederik Hayek's *Road to Serfdom*, which hurt him badly at the time of its publication in 1944 and which later became one of the key texts of the New Right revolution (Hayek, 1944).

I would not want to push the argument for Mannheim's contemporary relevance too far and, indeed, I shall go on to suggest that most of his own specific prescriptions are of little direct help to us today. Nevertheless, I agree with Colin Loader that 'if many of his answers can be rejected, the questions he raised...cannot' (1985: 189). For this reason, I have tried, in the chapters contained in this book, to continue the tradition of Mannheim by illustrating the importance of interrogating the 'common sense' not only of education policy but also educational research with the sort of lenses provided by sociology.

Today, just as in the days of Mannheim, too much education policy and a great deal of contemporary educational research has lost sight of Clarke's important insight that education policy needs to be informed by a sensitivity to the nature of the wider society. Mannheim himself was concerned about 'a tendency in democracies to discuss problems of organisation rather than ideas, techniques rather than aims' (1951: 199). However implicated universities may now have become in the instrumental rationality of the state, if they are not to be the places to explore the relationship between education and the wider social order, it is difficult to see where that work will be done on a sustained and systematic basis. Although the production of knowledge increasingly takes place in a whole variety of sites (Gibbons et al., 1994), there are some forms of knowledge production which are in danger of not taking place anywhere, since most of the other sites concerned with education are under even more pressure than we are to come up with 'quick-fix' solutions to immediate technical problems. This is an important part of the justification for the sort of analysis that is featured later in this book. For example, Chapters 2 and 3 provide contemporary examples of where I think sociology can help broaden our understanding of the complexity of educational interventions and our appreciation of what is at stake in them.

Classroom Discourse and Everyday Life

The first example, which features in Chapter 2, concerns the sociology of school knowledge. This was a field into which I was inducted by Basil Bernstein and Michael Young in my time as a student at the Institute in the late 1960s and early 1970s, but which I returned to in the 1990s through an empirical study of the implementation of cross-curricular themes, undertaken with Peter Aggleton and Gabrielle Rowe. Here I will offer just a brief glimpse of that work.

One of Mannheim's observations was that academic teaching had contributed to 'the suppression ... of ... awareness'. Over-specialisation had the effect of 'neutralizing the genuine interest in real problems and in the possible answers to them'. The student, he claimed, is 'rendered entirely uncritical by this method of teaching where everybody takes responsibility for a disconnected piece of [knowledge] only and is, therefore, never encouraged to think of situations as a whole' (Mannheim, 1943,: 65–6).

This has been an enduring concern in English education and was something that Denis Gleeson and I wrote about in the 1970s when we argued the need for a 'meaningful and critical' form of social education (Gleeson and Whitty, 1976). More recently, but rather late in the day, Kenneth Baker, Secretary of State for Education and Science in the Thatcher government, introduced cross-curricular themes as an antidote to the subject domination of his National Curriculum, supposedly to help pupils prepare 'for the opportunities, responsibilities and experiences of adult life' (Education Reform Act, 1988). The idea was that these themes would be taught mainly through the academic subjects using a permeation model.

Yet the research I undertook with Peter Aggleton and Gabrielle Rowe indicated that, while cross-curricular themes figured strongly in some very impressive and elaborate matrices being drawn up by senior management teams, the reality at classroom level was often very different. In practice, it was the subjects rather than the themes that were given prominence, and the boundaries between subjects and between school and non-school knowledge remained strong. Furthermore, the precarious existence of cross-curricular work was jeopardised by the low priority assigned to it by official curriculum and inspection agencies. This not only troubled progressive educators committed to developing a meaningful and critical approach to education, it also became a concern of the religious Right that the overemphasis on cognitive outcomes was marginalising the moral purposes of schooling so that children were not being taught traditional values.

So how might we make sense of this? Here, as can be seen in Chapter 2, what we found helpful was not so much the work of Mannheim himself, but that of Basil Bernstein, the first holder of the chair named after him. Although the roots of his own work derived more from Durkheim than Mannheim, his attempts to develop social theory surely exemplify what Sir Fred Clarke seemed to be asking for from a Professor of Sociology of Education. They help us to see, for example, that much education policy misrecognises the nature of the relationship between school and society. Probably Bernstein's most quoted dictum is that:

How a society selects, classifies, distributes, transmits and evaluates the educational knowledge it considers to be public, reflects both the distribution of power and the principles of social control.

This requires that we locate the study of curriculum change in 'the larger question of the structure and changes in the structure of cultural transmissions' (Bernstein, 1971: 47). At the heart of his own theory was an attempt 'to explicate the process whereby a given distribution of power and principles of control are translated into specialized principles of communication differentially, and often unequally, distributed to social groups/classes' (Bernstein, 1996: 93).

In our own example of cross-curricular themes, Bernstein's work on the classification and framing of educational knowledge and his writings on recognition and realisation rules and vertical and horizontal discourses (Bernstein, 1990, 1996, 2000) helped us to understand the formidable difficulties in switching between subjects and themes and, more importantly, what the wider implications are of doing so (Whitty et al., 1994a, 1994b). As Bernstein himself put it, 'attempts to change degrees of insulation reveal the power relations on which the classification is based and which it reproduces' (1996: 21).

Although subsequent debates about values in education and the community initiated by the School Curriculum and Assessment Authority and its successor go further towards recognising what is at stake than the earlier publications of the National Curriculum Council, they often seem equally naive about the extent to which schooling can compensate for society. Bernstein's work helps us to see that quick-fix solutions to enduring educational dilemmas, whether of a political or professional nature, are likely to have only limited impact and I would have to say that Mannheim himself might have learnt some useful lessons from Bernstein about this. I draw further on Bernstein's insights in Chapter 6 which, in discussing the overt and hidden curricula of marketised education systems, brings together my interest in the sociology of school knowledge with that in the sociology of education policy.

Devolution and Choice in Education

An example of my work in the sociology of education policy is featured in Chapter 3. This derives from research in which I have been engaged since the early 1980s, mainly with Tony Edwards, John Fitz, Sharon Gewirtz, Sally Power and David Halpin. It concerns the effects of devolution and choice in education.

Not surprisingly, given the time at which he was writing, Mannheim favoured some forms of selection in education. But he also questioned the view that 'struggle and social competition always foster and select those who are the best according to an absolute standard of worth'. In doing so, he contrasted 'objective abilities' with 'social abilities', including 'pulling strings and discovering influential patrons' (Mannheim, 1957: 85). While not dismissing the importance of competition, he saw the dangers of its going too far and stressed the necessity of cooperation. He also contrasted what he called 'the new democratic personalism' with 'the atomised individualism of the laissez-faire period' and emphasised the need to break down 'the frustration which comes from isolation, exaggerated privacy and sectarianism' and sought to mobilise instead 'the forces of group living in the service of a social ideal' (Mannheim, 1943: 52).

In recent years, in Britain and elsewhere, there have been concerted moves to create devolved systems of schooling entailing significant degrees of institutional autonomy and a variety of forms of school-based management and administration. In many cases, these changes have been linked to an increased emphasis on parental choice and on competition between diversified and specialised forms of provision, thereby creating 'quasi-markets' in educational services (Le Grand and Bartlett, 1993). Such policies received particular encouragement from New Right governments in Britain and the USA in the 1980s, and were subsequently fostered by the IMF and the World Bank in Latin America and Eastern Europe (Arnove, 1996). Even the political rhetoric of many parties of the centre left now places an increasing emphasis on diversity and choice in education, as is certainly the case with New Labour in Britain (discussed in the final two chapters of this book).

Most advocates of choice and school autonomy base their support on claims that competition will enhance the efficiency and responsiveness of schools and thus increase their effectiveness. Many hope that market forces will overcome a levelling-down tendency which they ascribe to bureaucratic systems of mass education, while others see them as a way of giving disadvantaged children the sorts of opportunities hitherto available only to those who can afford to buy them through private schooling or their position in the housing market (Moe, 1994; Pollard, 1995).

Yet, it will be clear from Chapter 3 (which updates Whitty, 1997) that my own reading of the evidence suggests that there is little hope of such dreams being realised in the absence of broader policies that challenge deeper social and cultural inequalities. Although recent changes in modes of social solidarity may not be as momentous as terms like post-Fordism and postmodernity suggest, there does seem to have been an intensification of social differences and a celebration of them in a new rhetoric of legitimation. As the new discourse of choice, specialisation and diversity replaces the previous one of common and comprehensive schooling, it is increasing the differences between popular and less popular schools on a linear scale – thereby reinforcing a vertical hierarchy of schooling types rather than producing the promised horizontal diversity. There is a significant body of evidence that, rather than benefiting the disadvantaged, this has the potential to exacerbate the disadvantage of those least able to compete in the market (Smith and Noble, 1995; Gewirtz et al., 1995; Lauder et al., 1994). For many members of disadvantaged groups, as opposed to the few individuals who escape from schools at the bottom of the status hierarchy, the new arrangements may prove to be just a more sophisticated way of reproducing traditional distinctions between different types of school and between the people who attend them.

It is too easy to accuse the perpetrators of such policies of bad faith. Even if there is some plausibility in the argument that handing decision-making down to schools and parents is a clever way of 'exporting the crisis', it is the misrecognition of the context that is more significant. As Amy Stuart Wells (1993a) points out, the economic metaphor that schools will improve once they behave more like private, profit-driven corporations and respond to the demands of 'consumers' ignores critical sociological issues that make the school consumption process extremely complex. Her own research in the USA suggests that escape from poor schools will not necessarily emerge from choice plans because 'the lack of power that some families experience is embedded in their social and economic lives' (Wells, 1993b: 48). Similarly, Gewirtz, Ball and Bowe (1992) suggest that, in the case of England, the new arrangements for school choice discriminate against those who have more pressing immediate concerns than being an educational 'consumer'. In their subsequent work (Gewirtz et al., 1995), they draw upon the theories of French sociologist Pierre Bourdieu (Bourdieu and Passeron, 1977) to explore 'the logic that informs the economy of cultural goods', which helps explain the class-related patterns of advantage and disadvantage they identify.

Sociology can thus help us to understand why, whatever the advocates of choice might believe, the mere provision of new choices to individual families is unlikely to overcome deep-rooted patterns of structural and cultural disadvantage. Changes, like the closing of the gender gap in education, arise from the interaction of a complex cluster of social and political forces (Arnot et al., 1999). Genuinely equal opportunities for all will only be achieved as part of a broader strategy of social and economic change. Indeed, Jean Anyon is probably right to argue that 'the only solution to educational resignation and failure in the inner city is the ultimate elimination of poverty and racial degradation' (1995: 89).

This means that there must be limits to the extent to which individual schools and their teachers can be expected to overcome these problems. Yet recent governments of both political hues in Britain, for example, have too often felt that the solution lies in the 'naming and shaming' of schools and teachers that do not live up to their expectations. Many of the strategies for 're-forming' the teaching profession, discussed in Chapter 4, can be seen when examined through the lenses of sociology as sometimes cynical, but more often misguided, attempts to 'shift the blame' for educational failure and growing inequality from the state to individual school managers and teachers.

Sociology and Educational Research

Much educational research, as well as education policy, remains stubbornly one-dimensional, uncritical and decontextualised (Ozga, 2000). Sociologists have often been particularly critical of work on school effectiveness and school improvement on this score. For example, the Australian sociologist of education, Lawrence Angus, criticises it for failing 'to explore the relationship of specific practices to wider social and cultural constructions and political and economic interests' (1993: 335).

As a result of their myopia, the more optimistic versions of work in this genre almost certainly exaggerate the extent to which local agency can challenge structural inequalities. Often it is not so much the specific claims, but rather the silences, that are significant here. It is interesting that this remains the case given that Clarke (1967: 167) justified the appointment of Mannheim to the Institute partly on the grounds that 'English theorizing about education... tended to take for granted the actualities of society when it did not ignore them completely'. Even today, as indicated in Chapter 7, some of the school effectiveness and school improvement literature conveniently glosses over the fact that one reading of the pioneering *Fifteen Thousand Hours* research (Rutter et al., 1979) is that, if all schools performed as well as the best schools, the stratification of achievement by social class could be even more stark than it is now.

Angus also suggests that a lack of engagement with sociological theory can mean that such work is trapped in 'a logic of common sense which allows it... to be appropriated into the Right's hegemonic project' (1993: 343). Thus it sometimes seems that not only neoliberal rhetoric, but also some forms of educational research, take the discursive repositioning of schools as autonomous self-improving agencies at its face value rather than recognising that, in practice, the atomisation of schooling too often merely allows advantaged schools to maximise their advantages. For those schools ill-placed to capitalise on their market position, the devolution of responsibility can lead to the devolution of blame.

In reality, though, many of the writers in this field do recognise such dangers. But Gerald Grace has pointed out that too often what Jenny Ozga (1990) terms the 'bigger picture' is not entirely ignored but alluded to in what he terms 'contextual rhetoric' at the beginning of a book or paper and then forgotten. The subsequent account may then still seem to exaggerate the degree to which and the circumstances in which individual schools and teachers can be empowered to buck the trends. It may thus raise unrealistic expectations which, when dashed, will only generate cynicism and low morale. For Grace, this makes such work an example of 'policy science', which excludes consideration of wider contextual relations 'by its sharply focused concern with the specifics of a particular set of policy initiatives...and is seductive in its concreteness, its apparently value-free and objective stance and its direct relation to action'. What risks being lost to view from this perspective is 'the examination of the politics and ideologies and interest groups of the policy making process; the making visible of internal contradictions within policy formulations, and the wider structuring and constraining effects of the social and economic relations within which policy making is taking place' (Grace, 1991: 26). This requires what he terms 'policy scholarship'.

However, I have always argued that it is not an 'either/or' issue. Good policy scholarship should subsume some of the more positive features of policy science but also go beyond it – as is evident in Grace's own work on school leadership (Grace, 1995) and on Catholic education (Grace, forthcoming). Certainly, some school effectiveness research would benefit by placing an increased emphasis on the policy scholarship dimension. Unless we constantly remind ourselves – and others – of both the possibilities and the limits of educational policy and practice, education researchers are liable to be misunderstood. For example, a critique by Peter Mortimore and Harvey Goldstein of a quasi-official research study by OFSTED was attacked in *The Observer* newspaper (27 October 1996) by Melanie Phillips. One of her arguments was that there was inconsistency between their claim that structural features of the three boroughs involved in the study helped explain the low levels of literacy of the pupils and other work by Mortimore that demonstrated that schools can make a difference. It did not seem to occur to Ms Phillips that both could be true, which they are, but the incident does demonstrate the importance in all our work of constantly keeping in view the 'bigger picture'. Chapter 7, parts of which originated in a joint paper with Peter Mortimore, in order to bring our two traditions of work closer together, can be seen as just such an attempt to locate work on school effectiveness and school improvement within a bigger picture informed by sociology.

The Sociological Imagination

A graphic, though perhaps unfortunate, metaphor for the role of sociology in educational studies might be a 'vulture's eye view' of the world. Apparently a vulture is always able to keep the background landscape in view while enlarging its object of immediate interest. However, the analogy does not quite capture the significance of the notion of the 'bigger picture'. The bigger picture is not just 'out there' in the background. As Giddens says of globalisation, it is not something that takes place beyond the local, it 'is an "in here" matter, which affects, or rather is dialectically related to, even the most intimate aspects of our lives' (1994b: 95). With regard to education, Jean Floud pointed out some time ago that this idea is central to the work of Bernstein and Bourdieu in demonstrating, in their different ways, 'integral links, even homologies, between the wider social structure and educational institutions and processes' (1977: 16).

Making the sorts of connections I am arguing for here involves understanding the intersection between biography and history, between identity and structure and between personal troubles and public issues – what C. Wright Mills (1961) termed the exercise of the 'sociological imagination'. Incidentally, Mills can indirectly be considered a student of Mannheim through his contact with his supervisor and collaborator, Hans Gerth, who had been an assistant to Mannheim in Heidelberg before moving to the University of Wisconsin at Madison in the USA.

For Mills, the exercise of the sociological imagination was not a feature of the work of all sociologists nor was it necessarily restricted to signed-up members of that profession. But even in a context of supposed 'reflexive modernisation' (Beck et al., 1994), there is too little evidence of it being exercised in contemporary institutional and political life. In these circumstances, I have to agree with Sir Fred Clarke's view that it is important for sociology to have a formal place in the study of education, if not with Mannheim's own more sociologically imperialist view that 'no educational activity or research is adequate in the present stage of consciousness unless it is conceived in terms of a sociology of education' (Mannheim and Stewart, 1962: 159). Unlike Martyn Hammersley (1996), I do not believe that sociologists of education should accept the demise of their discipline on the grounds that something like Giddens' 'double hermeneutic' (Giddens, 1984) has already taken a sociological way of thinking about the world into the common sense of other educators and educational researchers. We have only to reflect on the examples I have given here to recognise that too often this is just not the case. Furthermore, in the light of continuing attacks on theory within initial teacher training and teachers' professional development (see Furlong et al., 2000), Sir Fred Clarke's concerns may be even more pertinent than they were in the 1940s. Understanding the limits as well as the possibilities of action is an essential part of teachers' professional literacy, though some of the developments discussed in Chapters 4 and 8 may put its future at risk.

In the 1960s, Campbell Stewart (1967) commented that empirical sociologists of education had lost sight of the broader theoretical perspectives. My own view is that this is more generally true of educational research today. But am I therefore saying that *any* theory will do? Clearly, I have emphasised here theories that challenge a 'new common sense' in education policy and research that celebrates and exaggerates the extent to which all individuals and institutions have a realistic chance to grasp their own futures. Some other theories serve to bolster that common sense and, in doing so, help to legitimate and maintain existing relations of power. My own preference is for theories that provide a different set of lenses from those we take for granted. Yet we also need to recognise, like Mannheim, that those perspectives that give us a different 'take' on reality in one era can become part of the taken-for-grantedness of another. To that extent, there are some attractions in the advocacy by the current holder of the Karl Mannheim Chair of Sociology of Education, Stephen Ball, of the 'semiotic guerrilla warfare' of poststructuralist and deconstructionist views of the role of theory (Ball, 1995). However, like Mannheim, I am still committed to a version of the 'modernist' project in social research, though hopefully somewhat more reflexive about its own limits and possibilities than he was in his later years. But in interrogating theory with data and vice versa, I do want to claim that some theories are more powerful than others in helping us to see what is at stake in education and the limits and possibilities of professional and political interventions.

For example, as will be clear from Chapter 5, it seems to me that those versions of post-modernism that positively celebrate 'difference' and 'heterogeneity' serve to legitimate the rhetoric of reform, while those which emphasise 'distinction' and 'hierarchy' within a fragmented social order (Lash, 1990) provide a more adequate theorisation of its reality. Indeed, I myself would go further and argue, along with David Harvey (1989), that to regard the current espousal of heterogeneity, pluralism and local narratives as indicative of a new social order may be to mistake phenomenal forms for structural relations. In other words, postmodernist cultural forms and more flexible modes of capital accumulation may themselves be shifts in surface appearance, rather than signs of the emergence of some entirely new post-capitalist or even post-industrial society. To make policy on a different assumption may well be positively harmful.

Yet I do recognise that it is possible for such a perspective to lead to inaction rather than action. There have long been those who have criticised some forms of sociological theorising about education as generating total pessimism about the chances of things being different and thereby stripping teachers of any sense of agency. In that sense, the sort of sociology I am talking about might be seen to feed a Gramscian 'pessimism of the intellect'. Gerald Grace (1996) has made a similar point. Significantly, though, he went on to emphasise that policy scholarship could help to generate 'complex hope' rather than the 'simple hope' of the school improvement lobby – and thereby justify a more realistic degree of optimism of the will. This would seem to give sociology a responsible rather than an irresponsible role in relation to education policy.

Education Policy and Democratic Planning

It might, however, be argued that, although Grace's own notion of 'policy scholarship' is informed by a sense of both theory and history which helps us to recognise the 'bigger picture' within which educational policy and practice is located, the term itself reflects too much of a disarticulation between the concerns of the academy and those of the world beyond. Therefore I now want to consider whether there is any role for sociologists to move beyond diagnosis to prescription about possible interventions. Jean Floud has implied that Mannheim would have done better to continue 'to try to understand and diagnose, rather than to plan and legislate' (1959: 62). Although she had admired Mannheim when a student at the LSE and subsequently assisted him with his researches, Floud (1959) came to regard not only his view of the power of social science as suspect, but also his view of democracy. Following A. D. Lindsay, she claimed that, within a decade of his death, it was universally recognised that 'Mannheim's "planning for democracy"...was not "democratic planning"; and people were beginning to think in any case that "democratic planning" was a contradiction in terms...' (Floud, 1977: 8). But it does not seem to me that it is necessarily a contradiction in terms nor do I think we should eschew the task of considering how the rhetoric and reality of education might be brought into closer correspondence. However, I would no longer argue, even if I once did, that there is an imperative that requires all sociologists to make such a move.

Mannheim is probably best known for his idea of free-floating or socially unattached intellectuals. In the 1970s, sociologists of education often preferred to see themselves as the Gramscian organic intellectuals of the working class. Indeed, I myself confessed in an interview with Carlos Torres (1998) that there were times when I might have preferred to have held a chair named after Antonio Gramsci than Karl Mannheim. Increasingly, though, other sociologists of education have reconstituted themselves as Foucauldian specific intellectuals as the notion of a 'movement' to engage with has become difficult to sustain. Yet, while the sociology of education seems to have become more isolated in the academy and somewhat disengaged from wider social movements, grander theorists such as Anthony Giddens seem to be taking social theory back to its wider concerns and showing a willingness to try to address the political challenges posed by a changing social order. Giddens notes that 'on each side of the political spectrum today we see a fear of social disintegration and a call for a revival of community', but argues himself for the development of a 'dialogic democracy' in keeping with his analysis of the nature of the age and its attendant dangers (Giddens, 1994a: 124). Though he may not recognise it, this is a truly Mannheimian project, albeit one shorn of its confidence and certainty. In this contemporary form, which Giddens has subsequently sought to develop (Giddens, 1998), it could usefully be carried into sociological thinking about education policy.

However, we should also recognise that it is not only the sociology of education that has become disarticulated from its object of study or engagement. Using Bourdieu's notion of social field, James Ladwig (1994) argues that the field of education policy itself in the USA has developed a considerable degree of autonomy. He observes that the very fact that observations about the 'failure' of education policy or its implications for particular groups pose no threat to the relatively autonomous field of education policy is indicative of the extent to which education policy as a field has become self-justifying and self-perpetuating. The way in which governments declare policies a success and extend them even before they have been evaluated, and sometimes even before they have been implemented, is another example of this.

Unfortunately, though, Mannheim's own prescriptions do not provide us with a good model for rearticulating sociology with education policy and both with educational practice. For example, in his later writings advocating a revitalised conception of citizenship fostered through education for democracy, he seemed to forget some of the complexity of his earlier sociological work on generation units. Hoyle (1962) subsequently questioned how far Mannheim's consensual approach to social integration was feasible even in his own day and the increasing diversity of contemporary societies certainly makes his rather unidimensional proposals seem even more simplistic and problematic today.

Nevertheless, it should already be obvious from what I have said that I still regard sociological work as potentially relevant to educational policy and practice, at least in so far as it can help to make sense of the broader context of educational reform and demonstrate its utter complexity – even if it cannot prescribe action in any detail. This has some parallels with the view Mannheim expressed in *Ideology and Utopia*, where he wrote of political sociology that 'it must teach what alone is teachable, namely, structural relationships; the judgements themselves cannot be taught but we can become more or less adequately aware of them and we can interpret them' (Mannheim, 1936: 146).

In my earlier book *Sociology and School Knowledge*, I argued that 'one of the things that sociologists would almost certainly bring to such discussions [about policy and practice] would be a degree of caution, derived partly from...the study of past attempts at innovation' (Whitty, 1985: 176). However, I also suggested that 'the practical implications of [sociological] work for...political and educational practice [are] as much concerned with the ways in which policy is made as with specific substantive policies' (Whitty, 1985: 82). In this connection, it might seem appropriate to revive something like the wartime Moot in which Mannheim developed his ideas on planning and democracy. The Moot brought together a group of distinguished Christian laypeople and clergy with leading intellectuals, both Christian and non-Christian, at a series of residential weekends between 1938 and 1947, which came to focus on the postwar social and political reconstruction. It has been seen as an early think-tank, although in a fascinating recent paper about the Moot, William Taylor (1996) suggests that, rather like the All Souls Group with which it overlapped, it was closer to the model of a dining club or discussion group than a direct disseminator of policy proposals. Nevertheless, Mannheim became a key member – arguably the key member – of this particular group, as did Sir Fred Clarke, who took it upon himself to tease out the educational implications of Mannheim's general prescriptions about 'Planning for Freedom'. As a result, some of Mannheim's ideas can be seen to have indirectly influenced the 1944 Education Act (Clarke, 1967: 166).

Taylor suggests that 'democracy benefits when politicians, academics, administrators and professionals have opportunities to engage in policy debate away from their desks and in a context that requires neither agreed conclusions nor clear decisions'. He also says 'the ability of these informal groups to influence policy depends almost entirely on who they are able to attract as members'. Yet it seems to me that, for this day and age, groups like the wartime Moot and even the All Souls Group operate with an exclusive and rather patronising view of democracy. Even if Stewart (1967) and Loader (1985) may have been right to claim that critics such as Hoyle (1962, 1964) overstated the extent of Mannheim's elitism, the changes that have subsequently taken place in society now demand more radical conceptions of democracy – and they also demand more open discussion of what those alternatives might be. We still need to move beyond the 'old' politics of education and open up deliberation and decision-making to excluded constituencies. Similar sentiments underlie the demands for 'democratic professionalism' discussed in Chapter 4.

Thatcherism in education, as elsewhere, was partly successful because whole constituencies felt excluded from the social democratic settlement of the postwar era. Indeed, it appealed to them over the heads of 'bureau-professionals' who were characterised as having got fat by controlling other people's lives in the name of rationality and progress. Through its policies of 'devolution', Mrs Thatcher's government was able to characterise itself as democratic and the liberal educational establishment as elitist and engaged in restrictive practices behind closed doors.

Not that Thatcherism actually established 'deep democracy', of course. Within education, decisions have come to be made by groups that are even less democratically rooted than those they have replaced. Whatever the rhetoric of devolution may suggest, it is quite clear that significant constituencies have remained excluded from education policy and decision-making either intentionally or, just as often, as an unintended consequence of decisions made with the best of intentions. The result, as I implied earlier, is that market-oriented reforms may merely enable advantaged schools and advantaged families to enhance their advantages. This suggests that, if equity and social cohesion are to remain important considerations within education policy, there is an urgent need to balance consumer rights with a new conception of citizen rights to give voice to those excluded from the benefits of both social democratic and neoliberal policies.

I argue in Chapter 5 that, in so far as social relations are becoming increasingly accommodated in the notion of the strong state and the free economy (Gamble, 1988), neither the state nor civil society is currently much of a context for active democratic citizenship through which social justice can be pursued. The reassertion of citizenship rights in education would seem to require the development of a new public sphere somehow between the state and a marketised civil society, in which new forms of collective association can be developed. The real challenge is how to move away from atomised decision-making to the reassertion of collective responsibility for education, but without recreating the sort of over-centralised planning favoured by Mannheim.

If new approaches to collective decision-making are to be granted more legitimacy than previous ones, careful consideration will need to be given to the composition, nature and powers of new institutional forms if they are to prove an appropriate way of reasserting democratic citizenship rights in education in the twenty-first century. They will certainly need to respond to critiques of conventional forms of political association in most modern societies. While market forms are part of a social text that helps to create new subject positions which undermine traditional forms of collectivism, those forms of collectivism themselves often failed to empower many members of society, including women and minority ethnic groups.

In seeking to avoid the atomisation of educational decision-making, and associated tendencies towards fragmentation and polarisation between schools and within schools, we need to create new collective contexts within civil society for determining institutional and curricular arrange-ments that are genuinely inclusive. These will need to reflect a conception of citizenship that entails creating unity without denying specificity (Mouffe, 1989, 1992). Arguably, having a National Curriculum and devolved decision-making does at least recognise both parts of this requirement, but we have to find more adequate ways of doing so. Some of the discussions at the Moot about structures and values remain of interest in this connection, but such difficult public issues now need to be confronted publicly rather than in private.

The Left has so far done too little to develop an approach to public education which looks significantly different from the state education so often criticised in the past for its role in reproducing and legitimating social inequalities (Young and Whitty, 1977). Even if the social democratic era looks better in retrospect, and in comparison with neoliberal policies, than it did at the time, that does not remove the need to rethink what might be progressive policies for the new century. If we do not take the opportunity to do this, we may even find the policy agenda dominated by those radical rightist commentators who will foster the very forms of individualism and competition that Mannheim saw as such a threat to the future of liberal democracies.

This might involve moving still further towards marketised and even privatised forms of education provision. Indeed, some advocates of market forces have argued that the indifferent performance of the reforms to date is merely evidence that they have not gone far enough. James Tooley (1995), for example, favours an even more deregulated system and the abandonment of a centrally prescribed curriculum. He also claims that the potential of markets in education cannot be properly assessed by looking at the effects of quasi-markets or what he prefers to term 'so-called' markets. He is right, of course, to remind us of the equity failings of democratic systems, but as Smith and Meier (1995) pointed out in response to Chubb and Moe (1990), the failings of existing forms of democratic governance may necessitate reforming them rather than abandoning them.

Regrettably, our fascination with recent neo-liberal reforms may have blinded us to the potential of other ways of struggling to improve the education of disadvantaged groups. As James Henig rightly said of a similar situation in the USA, 'the sad irony of the current education-reform movement is that, through over-identification with school-choice proposals rooted in market-based ideas, the healthy impulse to consider radical reforms to address social problems may be channeled into initiatives that further erode the potential for collective deliberation and collective response' (1994: 222).

Towards a New Agenda?

If as a society we are thus in danger of being captured – or even trapped – by the discourse of marketisation (Bowe et al., 1994), sociologists may have a useful role in pointing to other possibilities. Indeed, it may be time to try to develop what Erik Olin Wright (1995) terms 'real utopias'. Wright, who works at the University of Wisconsin in Madison, which coincidentally is one of the American universities to which Mannheim himself nearly went rather than going to London, takes the view that 'what is pragmatically possible is not fixed independently of our imaginations, but is itself shaped by our visions'. His own Real Utopias Project works through 'utopian ideals that are grounded in the real potentials of humanity', but also with 'utopian destinations that have accessible waystations' and 'utopian designs of institutions which can inform our practical tasks of muddling through in a world of imperfect conditions for social change' (1995: ix). Even though Mannheim was suspicious of many forms of utopianism and said, in *Man and Society in an Age of Reconstruction*, that '"Planning" is not utopian; [because] it accepts the historically determined present state of society as its datum' (Mannheim, 1940), this formulation itself suggests that he might not have been averse to Wright's notion of 'real' utopias.

There has been a great deal of discussion about ways of democratising the state and civil society short of major constitutional changes. Mike Geddes (1996), for example, sees the future in terms of attempts to combine the virtues of different approaches to democracy. In particular, he seems to favour combining elements of representative and participatory democracy, by such devices as decentralising the policy process and establishing community councils, citizens' juries and opinion panels. However, in view of the lack of a firm constitutional basis for most such innovations, they tend to create ambiguity about whether they constitute democratic involvement in decision-making or mere consultation. Nevertheless, they may act as seedbeds for new ideas about democratic governance and contexts for Gramscian prefigurement struggles. Similarly, in the USA, Joshua Cohen and Joel Rogers (1995) take the view that it is possible to improve the practical approximation, even of market societies, to egalitarian democratic norms. They argue that, by altering the status of 'secondary associations' within civil society, associative democracy can 'improve economic performance and government efficiency and advance egalitarian-democratic norms of popular sovereignty, political equality, distributive equity and civic consciousness' (1995: 9).

I hope we can now develop new democratic forums in which to examine such ideas further and their implications for education policy-making. But rather than explore them in the sort of context in which Mannheim tried out his own ideas, we need to develop a more democratised version of the Moot – perhaps employing the new media. It may even be that the Internet has a role to play here, though I am by no means convinced that it is by definition a democratic medium and we would need to be as alert as Mannheim was in the case of other media to its totalising and totalitarian possibilities (Mannheim, 1943).

Significantly, the New Labour government of Tony Blair in Britain has established a National Grid for Learning, a government-sponsored portal giving access to officially approved educational websites. Advocacy of Information and Communications Technologies as a major source of educational progress and as a means of overcoming the democratic deficit has been an important feature of New Labour's rhetoric. As Selwyn (1999) points out in an early sociological assessment of this policy, the reality may prove rather different. The failure to acknowledge the complexity of the issues involved, which relate closely to those concerning the hidden and overt curricula discussed in Chapter 6, is a further illustration of some of the more worrying tendencies in New Labour education policy that I identify in an essay on the politics of education policy in Chapter 8. There, as well as discussing the educational record of the Blair government, I suggest that it has sometimes been as dismissive of the insights of policy scholarship in education as its Conservative predecessors.

Nevertheless, a number of high-profile sociologists, most notably Anthony Giddens, have become close to New Labour. Like his LSE forebear, Karl Mannheim – but with no direct reference to him – Giddens (1998) has written about a 'Third Way'. While Mannheim's 'Third Way' lay between a laissez-faire society and totalitarianism (Mannheim, 1951), Giddens' own version of the notion is an alternative to conventional social democracy and neo-liberalism. He suggests it is time to move beyond the old dualism of left and right. His Third Way is thus not just a mid-point between two political ideologies, but involves the creation of a new and heterodox alignment of ideas which recognises that our 'new times' may render many former political certainties obsolete. He believes New Labour is already moving in that direction and looks to Blair's leadership for a new version of government that will renew civil society through greater transparency and experiments with democracy. This could revive the notion of community, as well as creating a new mixed economy through the synergies of public, private and voluntary sectors. In doing so, it would transcend both the egalitarianism of the old left and the acceptance of inequality by the new right and replace these with the concept of social inclusion.

Nevertheless, particularly for the purposes of a Labour Party that still includes social democrats, and even a few democratic socialists, the Third Way is sometimes presented as a modernisation of social democracy to meet the needs of the 'new times'. It will, however, be clear from Chapter 8 that I am sceptical about the extent to which the reality, as opposed to the rhetoric, of New Labour's education policy yet lives up to its claims to be either the legitimate heir of social democracy or the harbinger of a distinctive new Third Way. Although some social democratic rhetoric has been revived by New Labour, there can be little doubt that in practice Tony Blair's own version of the Third Way is actually skewed heavily to the right.

There are some New Labour education initiatives that have, at least in principle, been seen to constitute something closer to Giddens' version of the Third Way. These include Education Action Zones (EAZs), heralded as 'standard bearers in a new crusade uniting business, schools, local education authorities and parents to modernise education in areas of social deprivation' (DfEE, 1998). The policy looks, at first sight, rather like a throwback to earlier attempts to use positive discrimination to tackle low educational achievement in areas of multiple disadvantage, such as the Educational Priority Areas of the 1960s and 1970s. On the other hand, it also contains organisational and managerial features that bear a closer resemblance to Conservative initiatives, such as Enterprise Zones, Urban Development Corporations and City Technology Colleges, while its critics have argued that the real purpose of EAZs is as a 'trojan horse of privatisation' (Socialist Teachers Alliance, 1998). EAZs seem to involve then both a reassertion of collective responsibility for educational provision and a readiness to consider the active involvement of private (even 'for profit') companies in its delivery. And, although the government has abandoned the Assisted Places Scheme in order to uphold its commitment to 'benefit the many, not the few', it has sought to bring private and state schools into closer partnership. It might appear, therefore, that EAZs entail an eclectic mix of new right and old left ideas, but (as in much of the New Labour reform agenda) with a preference for the business-oriented approaches introduced by the Conservatives.

However, it is also possible to argue that EAZs, and more specifically, their Education Action Forums, prefigure a new, more inclusive politics of education and fulfil Giddens' (1998: 79) vision of Third Way politics working at community level to provide practical means of furthering the social and material refurbishment of local areas. On this reading, EAZs could be regarded as one of those 'experiments with democracy' envisaged by Giddens as part of the way forward for public services in the twenty-first century (Halpin, 1999; Ranson, 2000). In theoretical terms, the EAZ policy might be located within the currently fashionable 'social capital' theories (e.g. Putnam, 1993), which suggest that interventions that increase 'social capital' can lead to consequent improvements in the educational achievement and economic prosperity of individuals who live in disadvantaged circumstances.

Despite this potential, New Labour has so far done relatively little to emphasise these aspects of EAZs. Indeed, our own research in some of the early zones suggests that enhanced community involvement on tradi-tional lines, let alone the fostering of new forms of civic association, has been distinctly limited. Managerialism and attempts to involve the private sector have been rather more prominent, although the latter strategy has met with only mixed success (Hallgarten and Watling, 2001; Dickson et al., 2001). Furthermore, some of the government's pronouncements about EAZs seem based not on the notion of 'positive welfare' preferred by Giddens, but on a deficit model of local communities and 'problem' parents and children (Gewirtz, 1998, 1999). Thus, even in EAZs, New

Labour's education programme has sometimes seemed, in practice, to follow the path of the New Right in preference both to that of the old left and a distinctive new way forward. This might not matter too much if, as is often argued, the mark of New Labour's Third Way is a healthy pragmatism based on 'what works' and it could deliver the reduction of educational inequalities that, as shown in Chapter 7, has eluded earlier initiatives. However, the scale of resources for EAZs is very small proportionately to the overall education budget (Plewis, 1998) and certainly does not meet the case set out in that chapter for the significant redistribution that would be needed to make a substantial and sustained impact on social and educational disadvantage.

It is, of course, too early to predict with any confidence the ultimate outcomes of New Labour's programme of educational reform. While democratising and socially inclusive aspects of its policies are as yet relatively underdeveloped, there have been suggestions that they will figure more prominently in its second term. Certainly, as I argue in Chapter 8, there is an urgent need to counter the polarisation and social exclusion associated with the more atomised version of educational quasi-markets. Provided we do not abandon these aspirations as 'unrealistic', but accept that we can only work towards them from where we are now, then a 'Third Way' that is closer in spirit to Mannheim's may eventually come back on the agenda.

Conclusion

Campbell Stewart once said of Mannheim that 'before long we shall need again to call on the kind of perspective which [he] could command and which for the moment we seem too committed [to other priorities] to realize we have lost' (1967: 37). Interestingly, Chris Woodhead (1998), England's former Chief Inspector of Schools, has also called for a return to the traditions of Mannheim's time. He used a review of the reissued sociology of education volumes in Mannheim's International Library of Sociology to attack contemporary education research in general and the sociology of education in particular and to contrast the latter's present standing with the 'intellectual high ground it occupied when Karl Mannheim began putting his library together' (1998: 52). Woodhead even called for a 'third way' for the sociology of education, as an alternative to what he characterised as 'the ethnomethodological road' and the 'macro-explanatory' route, although in my view this dichotomous characterisation of the field probably applies more to the 1970s and 1980s than to the present day. Nevertheless, it should be clear from this book that I agree with Michael Young (1998a: 31) who, while pointing to some obvious limitations and contradictions in Woodhead's analysis, has conceded that 'education research has certainly got to ask some hard questions about its methodology, concepts and priorities and...its links with teachers and policymakers'. But I hope it will also be clear that the sociology of education has not entirely abandoned what Woodhead characterises as its 'classical terrain' and that contemporary sociology of education can still make a useful contribution to understanding and developing education policy.

Further Reading

Demaine, Jack (ed.) (1999) *Education Policy and Contemporary Politics*. London: Macmillan.
Demaine, Jack (ed.) (2001) *Sociology of Education Today*. London: Palgrave.
Mannheim, Karl (1951) *Freedom, Power and Democratic Planning*. London: Routledge & Kegan Paul.

Notes

1. Since I assumed the Directorship of the Institute, Stephen Ball has been appointed to the Karl Mannheim Chair.
2. In Chapter 2, I similarly utilise some of Bernstein's later work to try to make sense of an aspect of policy related to my earlier interest in the school curriculum.

2

School Knowledge and Social Education
with Peter Aggleton and Gabrielle Rowe

This chapter draws upon the concepts of Basil Bernstein, first holder of the Karl Mannheim Chair of Sociology of Education at the Institute of Education, to explore the complex relationship between curricular knowledge and everyday life. More specifically, it reports on an empirical study of the teaching of cross-curricular themes in English secondary schools in the 1980s. The analysis helps to explain some of the difficulties encountered in implementing the Thatcher government's attempts to use a subject-based National Curriculum to prepare pupils for particular aspects of adult life.

Section One of the landmark Education Reform Act 1988 required schools to provide a balanced and broadly based curriculum which 'promotes the spiritual, moral, cultural, mental and physical development of pupils ...and...prepares such pupils for the opportunities, responsibilities and experiences of adult life'. However, the Act introduced a mandatory National Curriculum defined in terms of academic subjects. These 'core and other foundation subjects' were identified as English, mathematics, science, technology, history, geography, modern languages, music, art and physical education (PE). Schools were subsequently advised to teach five non-mandatory 'cross-curricular themes' – namely health education, citizenship, careers education and guidance, economic awareness, and environmental education.[1] The guidance issued by the then National Curriculum Council (NCC, 1990a) suggested that, although these themes could be taught in a variety of ways and discrete provision might prove necessary for certain elements, most aspects of the themes could be taught through the core and other foundation subjects or through religious education (RE).

Official comments on the relationship between subjects and themes reflected an ambivalence about two contrasting traditions of social education in the English secondary school curriculum. The social education of the elite has usually been based upon a 'liberal education' in a variety of academic subjects, while that of the masses has often taken the form of direct preparation for citizenship and work. The traditional notion of a 'liberal education' assumes that exposure to a broad range of specialist subject discourses will produce an 'educated person'. Such a person will then, almost by definition, be an employable, environmentally friendly, responsible citizen and taxpayer, pursuing a healthy lifestyle. From this point of view, it makes sense for the cross-curricular themes to be taught through the core and other foundation subjects. For schools, it relieves pressure on the curriculum to cater directly for every fashionable political imperative. It also seems to provide a way of meeting such demands, while avoiding charges of 'indoctrination' and 'social control' often associated with more explicit attempts to prepare pupils for adult life through citizenship and vocational education (Gleeson and Whitty, 1976; Whitty, 1985).

However, the 'permeation' approach to the teaching of the cross-curricular themes assumes that subjects and themes are essentially different ways of organising the same curricular elements. It also assumes that the same elements can be used for different educational purposes at the same time. For example, health education may involve the acquisition of subject knowledge and understanding, the development of life skills associated with the making of sound choices, and the fostering and adoption of particular attitudes and lifestyles. Yet, each of these different educational purposes entails different criteria of quality and this has important implications for the nature of classroom activity and associated modes of assessment. Traditional secondary school subjects tend to privilege the acquisition of knowledge and understanding. There are therefore likely to be tensions between provision for subjects and themes in the secondary school curriculum. The Thatcher government's view that the educational aims associated with themes could easily be achieved by mapping them on to mainstream subjects was either naive or cynical.

Indeed, the inherent difficulties of the permeation approach to social education have been exacerbated in the case of the cross-curricular themes by a concurrent narrowing of what counts as knowledge in mainstream school subjects as a result of the work of the National Curriculum subject working parties and interventions by successive Secretaries of State. The NCC's claim that, in due course, it is likely that schools will 'throw all the attainment targets in a heap on the floor and reassemble them in a way which provides for them the very basis of a whole curriculum' (NCC, 1990a: 1), fails to acknowledge that the particular attainment targets identified by the subject working parties have mainly been driven by the requirements of individual academic subjects.

This chapter draws upon the findings of a research project, which involved a survey of one in four secondary schools in England and Wales (N = 1,431) and detailed observation in eight schools.[2] It demonstrates that, in both teaching and assessment, criteria of quality associated with individual academic subjects have generally taken precedence over those that might have been used to evaluate the rather broader notion of social education that seemed to be implied in Section One of the 1988 Act. In doing so, it also points to some more general issues that will need to be faced in any attempt to develop an approach to social education that combines rigour and relevance.

The study was informed theoretically by Basil Bernstein's work on the classification and framing of educational knowledge (Bernstein, 1971). Bernstein originally defined 'classification' as 'the *relationship* between contents', so that 'where classification is strong, contents are well insulated from each other by strong boundaries [and] where classification is weak... the boundaries between contents are weak or blurred' (Bernstein, 1971: 49). The concept of 'framing' referred to the 'strength of the boundary between what may be transmitted and what may not be transmitted, in the pedagogical relationship'. Where there is strong framing, 'there is a sharp boundary, where framing is weak, a blurred boundary, between what may and may not be transmitted' (Bernstein, 1971: 50).

A curriculum comprised of individual subjects with strong classification between contents was described by Bernstein as a 'collection code'. He suggested that the traditional subject-based English grammar school curriculum approximated to this model, but that there had been moves during the 1960s and 1970s towards what he termed 'integrated codes' – where there was weaker classification between subjects, for example through the development of integrated humanities courses (Whitty, 1992b). However, it seemed to us that the Education Reform Act's model of the National Curriculum favoured a strongly classified subject curriculum – that is, a reassertion of the collection code. The subsequent detailed specification of official programmes of study for the core and other foundation subjects also seemed to herald a strengthening of 'framing' in Bernstein's terms, especially in view of his statement that 'where framing is strong, then the acquirer has little control over the selection, organization and pacing of the transmission' (Bernstein, 1977: 179).

Yet, the very idea of using cross-curricular themes as a basis for social education, as proposed in the National Curriculum Council's various booklets of non-statutory guidance on the themes, seemed to require a weakening of the boundaries between subjects and entail a weakening of framing in the pedagogic relationship as a result of the need to relate school knowledge to pupils' own lifestyles and concerns. We were therefore interested to see how these apparent tensions between different models of curriculum and pedagogy, and their associated modes of assessment, would actually be resolved in school policy and classroom practice.

The National Survey

Our questionnaire asked headteachers or their curriculum deputies whether their schools had made changes in cross-curricular policy and practice following the NCC Guidance on themes in 1990. By the time of our survey in 1992, 82 per cent of schools claimed to have changed their approach. One-third of these stated that the change was due to the National Curriculum, but about a quarter attributed the change to developments of previous practice and were keen to make it clear that change was internally generated and not entirely due to NCC Guidance. However, 84 per cent of all those who had changed their approaches claimed to have referred to the NCC guidance documents.

The questionnaire responses showed teaching of the various themes to be spread across the core and other foundation subjects in different ways. Some heads ticked every subject on the grounds that themes were by definition permeated. But most were somewhat more discriminating in their responses and the responses as a whole showed different patterns for the different themes. When we looked at the areas in which at least 50 per cent of schools claimed to be teaching the themes, we found that economic and industrial understanding appeared in the most subjects, and could thus be defined as the most fully permeated theme, whereas health education and careers education and guidance were the least permeated of the themes.[3]

Health education and careers education were also those themes having the clearest visibility in schools. They had existed long before they were defined as cross-curricular themes and they were more likely than the others to have discrete curriculum slots or be part of a Personal and Social Education (PSE) programme. Even when this was not the case, they tended to be taught through relatively few core and foundation subjects. They were also more likely than the other themes to have written policies and were among those most likely to have designated co-ordinators backed by a responsibility allowance. In recent years, they had been supported by nationally funded advisory teachers. Thus, health and careers had some of the attributes in terms of status, time and resources that Ivor Goodson and others have argued are necessary to 'becoming a school subject' (Goodson, 1983, 1985). The closer a theme was to a conventional subject in these respects, the stronger and more tangible its presence seemed to be. It seems from our findings that those themes (i.e. health and careers) which Don Rowe (1993) has suggested are *least* like academic subjects in terms of their substance are also those *most* likely to have the some of the key sociological attributes of subjects.

This has implications for the capacity of these themes to employ distinctive criteria of quality in that it seems likely that having some of the attributes of a subject in terms of its form may allow a theme to deviate from other subjects in terms of its substance. Thus, for example, health educators and careers educators often pride themselves on the links they make to everyday life, on their participatory approaches to learning and on their concern with affective as well as cognitive outcomes. They also tend to make more extensive use of pupil self-evaluation techniques than most other school subjects. The opportunities they have to do these things may actually be dependent upon the relative insulation of their work from the rest of the curriculum and their occupation of curriculum slots in their own right. In Bernstein's terms, their capacity to maintain weak framing in the classroom and weak boundaries in relation to the outside world may result from their strong classificatory relationships with other subjects. As Graham Fowler (1992) points out in relation to liberal studies in post-compulsory education, weak framing is acceptable in an area of work strongly differentiated from other subjects only because the dangers of polluting high-status knowledge are thereby minimised.

However, the opportunities for careers and health education to maintain their unusual character, either in their own right or in the context of PSE, are far from secure. As well as our own research, there is other evidence that the time allowance for these activities has been eroded or threatened in many schools by the pressure of curriculum overload brought about by the National Curriculum (HEA, 1992; S. Harris, 1993). Their survival as themes is therefore increasingly dependent upon the adoption of a permeation approach, which is likely to emphasise those aspects of their work which are closest in substance to mainstream school subjects.

Where the teaching of a theme relies on a permeation model, any distinctive features are likely to become casualties at classroom level of the strong classification and strong framing associated with conventional academic subjects, which are now being reinforced by the demands of the subject-based National Curriculum. Don Rowe (1993) suggests the other three themes are less different than health and careers from mainstream subjects in their substance and it may be that there is less of a problem in those cases. Yet, even if he is right that the knowledge content of those themes is closer to that of other subjects, the purposes to which it is to be put still differ and this is likely to have consequences for the criteria by which it is to be assessed.

The 'Permeation' Model in Practice

The second phase of our project involved visiting eight secondary schools identified as having different approaches to cross-curricular work. Briefly, the themes were not much in evidence in the work we saw, even in those schools that claimed to have given them some priority in whole-school curriculum planning. Most schools were feeling constrained by the pressures of the National Curriculum to adopt an approach that put an increasing emphasis on the delivery of themes via the core and other foundation subjects with RE. When we looked at what was going on in those subjects, we found that the newer themes, and even the older themes where a permeation model was being adopted, were difficult to identify at classroom level and they were rarely 'visible' to pupils.

We have tried to make sense of what we saw in terms of Bernstein's work on evoking contexts, recognition rules and realisation rules (Bernstein, 1981). Different contexts evoke different responses and one of the marks of competence is knowing the rules that enable you to produce appropriate responses in a particular context. According to Bernstein, 'recognition rules create the means of distinguishing between and so *recognising* the speciality that constitutes a context' (Bernstein, 1990: 15). In our context, recognition rules may be the clues which pupils need to determine what counts as a specialised discourse, in other words a subject. One of the first recognition rules derives from how subjects or themes are divided up. Other salient clues for novices are gained through having to bring specialist equipment such as books, aprons and sports kits to some lessons. Other recognition rules will be given by what form or forms school work takes. Of particular importance when considering themes are the recognition rules which govern talk. These are given either explicitly or tacitly through the rules of classroom discourse. Teachers at the beginning of a year often tell pupils what, in general terms, constitutes acceptable talk.

Realisation rules are the rules which tell pupils what constitutes appropriate practice in a lesson. In Bernstein's terms, 'realisation rules regulate the creation and production of specialized relationships internal to the context' (Bernstein, 1990: 15). They tell pupils what can and what cannot be done to demonstrate knowledge. They suggest acceptable forms in which subject principles may be demonstrated and this is particularly important in the context of assessment. Realisation rules give the form that pupils' written work may take, acceptable methods of oral communication, types of movement in PE and forms of artefact which may be produced in technology and art. More sophisticated realisation rules may refer to the structure of arguments or the acceptable sequences of a process.

During lessons teachers will control discourse in order to demonstrate what can literally be said and not said according to the subject code. Sometimes the parameters, or form, of the discourse are given explicitly, as for example with the rules of a formal debate, and sometimes pupils infer them, as for example when talking individually with a teacher. As pupils become used to the ways of working in a subject, they will start to take teachers' accepted discourse rules for granted. When pupils break these tacit rules, teachers will be forced to articulate them again and they will, for a period, become visible.

One of the key problems about using subjects to teach themes lies in the rules that relate to the use of talk in different contexts. We found that all pupils made a strong distinction between subject discourses and talk which they perceived as not directly related to subjects. We asked pupils 'Where do you do a lot of talking?' They indicated that most talk took place during breaks and lunch time. This sort of 'chat' associated with peer group and family contexts was clearly differentiated from school work. When 'chat' did take place in lessons, it had an illicit feel to it, as these comments by pupils indicate:

Yeah, it's good. It takes up most of the lessons. It's not really doing English.

(School A)

Depends which subject you can't really concentrate on.

(School A)

We can chat in Art, he chats, he gets side-tracked very easily.

(School B)

We do a lot of talking in Graphics, in Graphics we just mess around and talk a lot.

(School B)

Unless you enjoy the lesson, you just sit there and talk.

(School C)

In CDT we make things but it could get boring so we talk – not to do with the lesson.

(School D)

'Chat' is thus often associated with time out or off task. Pupils perceive it as something to 'get away with' or 'side-tracking' and therefore not related to the subject. Unlike teacher talk, question and answer sessions and structured discussion, it is seen as subverting rather than contributing to learning. The problem facing themes is that the sort of talk that allows links to be made between subject discourses and everyday life challenges this strong boundary between legitimate school talk and illegitimate non-school talk. Themes can therefore create ambiguity about the status and permissibility of different types of talk – in the eyes of pupils as well as those of some teachers.

Furthermore, those very types of talk that attempt to forge connections between school talk and 'street talk', and which are therefore important to the effective teaching of themes, are valued differentially by different subjects. What counts as legitimate talk varies from subject to subject. Some pupils are able to differentiate subjects according to whether or not, and in what ways, oral work is legitimate. Our focus-group interviews with pupils asked them to differentiate the different types of talk which take place in subjects:

> Don't get people to join in the conversation so much in science, they just write on the board and then talk about it. Then he just explains how the experiment works. Then in English he asks about the book you are reading. Not so much writing on the board. It's discussing.
>
> In English you have more debates.

(School G)

> *Right, what are you talking about in your biology lesson?*
>
> About the work we've done really to see if we've taken it all in.
>
> *Right, so it's very work-orientated talk rather than chat?*
>
> Yeah.
>
> *Is it like a debate?*
>
> No, it's either yes or no.

(School B)

These pupils recognised in which subjects there was a place for their own views and ideas and in which subjects these were not validated. They thus recognised differences in framing between different subjects.

Where classroom discourse is tightly framed, teachers will be perceived by pupils to be in complete control of what is said. One example is when teachers limit pupils' contributions to answering closed questions. However, tight framing can have the effect of making recognition rules more explicit, because it makes the limits of common-sense understanding clear. Pupils will then be able to work out that answers based on common-sense, rather than on subject principles, are not given credit. However, if the framing is too tight some pupils may not be able to connect subject principles with any of their own ideas and the subject principles may simply elude them.

If the discourse rules are much looser, a great deal of what pupils say may be accepted, but it will be more difficult for them to work out what the specialist area of knowledge is. However, in some cases, teachers themselves use loose framing to work out what lay theories pupils already hold in a subject area. Once they have worked out what lay theories pupils hold they can then use this, as scaffolding in Bruner's sense (Bruner and Haste, 1987), to introduce a subject principle. This can provide a 'relevant' context through which to illustrate a principle.

Teachers often like to use examples which they hope are familiar to pupils in order to provide contexts through which they can demonstrate subject principles. In many cases, though, these apparently 'real' examples are not drawn directly from pupils at all and are actually at some variance with pupils' experience of everyday life. Some pupils therefore find it difficult to make sense of either the principles or the examples (Keddie, 1971; Noss, 1990; Cooper, 1992). Another way to use pupils' understanding is to show how their common-sense theories conflict with the under-standing required to grasp the subject principle. Indeed Driver et al. (1985) suggest that unless teachers point out to pupils how their common-sense theories conflict with scientific theories, they may never acquire scientific principles.

However, if subjects are also to do the work implied by the permeation model of themes and help prepare pupils for life beyond school, yet another relationship between subject knowledge and common sense would be necessary. The subject principles would need to be related back to everyday life either by the pupils themselves or with the help of teachers. In the lessons we observed, this rarely happened, because the dominant 'realisation rules' in play were those of the subject. Furthermore, those pupils who had successfully learnt to differentiate subjects according to these rules were inhibited from making thematic links across subjects or beyond subjects to the world outside school.

During one year 10 science lesson about teeth and tooth decay in a school with a very clear permeation policy for cross-curricular themes on paper, we asked a pupil:

Don't you need to say something about how you should brush your teeth?

I don't think we're supposed to do that.

Why?

It's not what we're doing.

Why are you doing this work then?

Because it's in the National Curriculum, I suppose. (laughs)

But the textbook has a picture of how you should brush your teeth.

I don't think that's really science.

(School G)

For this pupil, even an illustration in the science textbook was not enough to legitimate a connection between the National Curriculum subject 'science' and everyday life. To him the science lesson was self-contained and self-referential. To have produced work inconsistent with what he perceived as the subject code would have indicated that, through inappropriate application of recognition and realisation rules, he had failed to achieve the required scientific competence. The task was thus perceived as one associated purely with scientific knowledge rather than with personal behaviour.

While the particular example may seem trivial, it clearly has wider implications for a permeation approach to, say, drugs or HIV education. Even explicitly participatory approaches to health education in other contexts have experienced considerable difficulties in forging links between knowledge and behaviour. Health educators' initial concern that the National Curriculum would concentrate unduly on factual knowledge at the expense of process skills and participatory learning styles were allayed to some extent by the NCC guidance for this theme (NCC, 1990b). Despite this, the classroom practice that we observed seemed to confirm their fear that quality in health education would be defined in relation to subject-specific attainment targets rather than the developmental needs of pupils or the responsibilities of adult life.

Ironically, the teacher of the particular science class reported here was a staunch advocate of cross-curricular themes and had a senior responsibility for the implementation of the whole school curriculum policy. He had earlier told us of his fear that the National Curriculum might make it difficult to link science to pupils' experiences and his own practice seemed now to provide evidence to support this thesis. Unfortunately, this was not an isolated instance. Furthermore, some science teachers, and particularly male science teachers, complained most strongly that teaching cross-curricular themes 'polluted' their subject. That explicit theme-related work is perceived as both residual and potentially threatening to the integrity of science as a subject is evident in this comment from one such teacher:

> There are occasions in science where things will crop up but probably not as often, but I mean we were doing some work on alcohol for instance this week in year 11…things can come up, even though what you're doing tends to be very much more structured in some science lessons, there are issues that do *intrude* and *if there's time* we can discuss them [our emphasis].
>
> (School C)

In a focus-group interview with teachers in another school discussing where themes are taught, a science teacher said of the themes:

> Not in key stage three, sorry, because you've got the National Curriculum document which you've got to wade through in a pre-set

time and I mean the Science department as a whole – I know Rob is responsible for economic awareness – we've done virtually nothing on that because if you're trying to get over a particular attainment target, and let's say you've allowed yourself one lesson or maybe two lessons to do that, then you want the *essential thread* to go through. Whereas y'know you've got to go off at a tangent sometimes to bring in economic awareness…what you're doing then is *diluting the message* [our emphasis].

(School D)

In yet another school the science teacher in the focus group interview stated about health education:

It's not our job at all. We do do it, but we shouldn't have to. Parents should do it. Our main aim is to get them through the exam. Social niceties are not really our…we're not nappy changers…nannies.

(School E)

To some extent, then, the teacher who taught the lesson about tooth decay was the exception, at least in his stated commitment to teaching themes and his worry that the National Curriculum would squeeze them out. Yet his practice did not differ significantly from those teachers who believed it was important to protect the purity of their subject. Science teachers seem to keep a strong control over the message and guard their position as subject specialists very tightly. While their tight control over the discourse alienates some pupils, it also has the effect of producing a discourse which pupils perceive as having strong rules and procedures which in Bernstein's terms provide recognition rules.

At the same time, many of these same teachers felt that themes, as opposed to subjects, benefited from their 'invisibility'. A teacher talking about economic and industrial understanding told us:

It has to be seen as part of the whole pattern rather than something that's taken out and emphasised. It occurs in so many places…you were talking about nineteenth-century history…it occurs in history …it occurs in literature; it's there in all of them, it's just there as the background, it's bound to be. I think we raise children's awareness but I don't think it should be a structured…should…what's the word…I don't think we should throw it at them…as lumps that…what they need to know…it should be kept in perspective …It doesn't kind of exist on its own. It permeates things.

(School G)

But this means that all theme-related knowledge forms only the background to subject principles. In Bernstein's sense, the themes are foregrounded by the subjects which are, in turn, strongly insulated from each other. If themes are to be effective, pupils themselves have to be able to make connections between any elements of the themes which they will have come across scattered around different subjects and apply this knowledge to life outside school – a complex set of cognitive and practical tasks.

Furthermore, Bernstein's work would suggest that some groups of pupils are likely to be better placed to make the connections than others. It certainly seems likely that relatively 'invisible' themes will only be put back together, or subject knowledge recontextualised, by pupils who are able to recognise an appropriate context for doing so and then apply yet another set of realisation and recognition rules that are different from those of individual subjects. This context may be a PSE lesson in school or it may be in the home or peer group. If the context is the home or is heavily home determined, then the opportunities to make sense of theme-related knowledge are likely to be differentially distributed according to social and cultural backgrounds.

During the fieldwork, questionnaires were administered to year 8 and year 10 pupils in some of the schools we visited. They asked if pupils had heard of each of the cross-curricular themes and then, separately, if they had been taught any of them. Initial analysis suggests that pupils do not 'see' a lot of what curriculum managers identify as theme-related work. But they are in broad agreement about which themes they have heard of and which they have been taught. In general they agree that they are taught careers education and guidance, health education and environmental education. Across the schools from which we have relevant data, relatively few pupils had heard of the term economic and industrial understanding or thought they were being taught any. The findings were similar for education for citizenship except in one school which had a specific citizenship module as part of a PSE programme.

However, the broad agreements among pupils appeared to break down when we asked them to explain briefly what they understood each of the themes to be. In focus group interviews, some pupils seemed to describe themes according to the conventions of subject discourses, using abstract principles, while others would describe them according to topic orientations which tended to be in the form of concrete examples. For example, some said that economic and industrial understanding was about about 'how the economy works' and others that it was about 'managing on your wages'.

We therefore investigated the reasons for the different ways in which pupils talked about the themes. If the work of Holland (1981) were to be replicated in this rather different context, we would expect middle-class children to prioritize abstract principles associated with subjects, with working-class children more likely to refer spontaneously to aspects of everyday life. We found that the extent to which there were actually significant differences between how pupils from different backgrounds described the themes varied from theme to theme. The most significant differences related to health education and economic and industrial understanding, where pupils from non-manual backgrounds were far more likely to discuss themes in context-independent language than those from manual backgrounds (Whitty et al., 1994b).

However, there were also some significant differences between schools in this respect. Not surprisingly, most of the pupils in a school which relied largely on teaching the themes through a highly academic subject-based curriculum described economic and industrial understanding in terms of concepts drawn from economics. Pupils in schools which adopted more varied approaches were more likely to characterise this theme in context-dependent terms and, in one school, there were no examples at all of context-independent language in relation to this theme.

Personal and Social Education (PSE)

Effective teaching of the themes requires movement between context-dependent and context-independent language. It is therefore important to find ways of enabling all pupils to make connections between the abstract knowledge associated with subjects and pupils' own experiences in everyday life. Some schools do try to offer pupils the possibility of learning about the themes elsewhere than in the core and other foundation subjects, though this is more true of some themes than others. PSE lessons or similar provision might constitute an important context for pupils to pull together all the subject-related knowledge associated with themes. Such provision could, in theory, help to counteract the differential social distribution of opportunities to do so outside school.

In fact, though, none of the PSE courses we observed during fieldwork even attempted to bring together theme-related subject knowledge in this way. Even the most highly organised schools did not attempt to relate PSE courses to other subject provision in a clear and coherent manner. Instead, if PSE was offered, the reason was to teach those aspects of themes which were not likely to be included in subjects. Such curriculum provision thereby took on the form of a 'subject' in its own right, strongly classified in relation to other subjects. However, if schools organise the teaching of themes in this way, it can no longer really be called 'cross-curricular' and the challenge of bringing together knowledge from different subject areas may be avoided rather than confronted.

PSE was as likely to suffer from its separation from other subjects as to benefit from it. Where PSE and similar lessons did not have clear recognition rules, there was a tendency for them not to be seen as 'proper' subjects and some pupils found it difficult to make sense of them. We asked pupils about PSE and other issues in the focus-group interviews:

Where do you discuss issues like moral issues?

We do that in PSE but it's much more boring [than in RE]. In PSE no one takes it seriously ... fall asleep.

Depends on the teacher. Mr Y they take the mick out of him. He talks and talks and never stops.

PSE is a 'catch-all' lesson. It takes in everything.

What is the difference in talk between PSE and English?

In PSE, it's always the practical things, how we ... it's always, how we could do it in the tutor group. Why our tutor group is like this. What can we do about it. They talk about how to solve it. They tell you it's there. In PSE they tell you how to get rid of it. Which is the problem.

I see it's a sort of practical thing?

Yeah.

It's more down to earth.

Whereas in a subject area ... like English ...

It's more depth in a subject really, you go into it more.

(School C)

For these pupils, PSE was perceived to be superficial and lacking a focus and even its concern with practical issues was seen in negative terms. Thus, although little attention was paid to the themes within subject classrooms, the teaching of the themes in a separate PSE lesson often merely confirmed their lowly status.

Part of the difficulty lies in the fact that in PSE there are no agreed conventions about how to frame the discourse. Potentially anything can be said and many teachers expressed anxiety about how to limit the talk. They were aware of having moral positions which would not necessarily be those of pupils and they were unsure about how much they could allow pupils to say in PSE lessons. Pupils themselves were aware of the rather arbitrary conventions governing PSE discussions and therefore perceived the limitations of what could and could not be said in PSE as personal attributes of the teachers.

The recognition of a lack of a perceptible PSE 'voice' was articulated by year 10 pupils in this extract from a focus-group interview:

> It's what they think personally. So, if they think it's really interesting then they want to talk about it. They really get into it, if not they'll probably just go quickly.

> It's because the teachers have had to work it out, all the course work. It's because in every school, everyone's doing it in totally different ways. The teachers have just sat down and worked, written out sheets, or whatever they are working from. If say, they were working from a text book say, and it's been developed over a period of time, I'm sure it would be better.

> I don't like PSE, have to swop round different teachers. You never know where you are. They don't tell you what you are doing.
>
> (School A)

The recognition rules which create areas of specialist meaning which are subjects, such as textbooks, homework and examinations, were clearly not available in this context.

Even when PSE was assessed, the assessment criteria appeared to be independent of any identifiable public discourse:

> If you sit there and look attentive, you'll get a good mark.

> Say, 'yeah' a lot.

> If you put your hand up often and give an intelligent comment.

> Get in the teacher's good books.

> Yeah, I did that the other day. I had to have a report filled in. I put my hand up and answered a question. She gave me an 'A'.
>
> (School C)

Here pupils explained how they manipulated the teacher to get good marks. In mainstream subjects it is not this easy because what counts as 'correct' or 'an intelligent comment' is distinguishable from incorrect or unintelligent answers according to subject conventions which are perceived to be more public or more formal, or at least they are thought to emanate from a source other than the individual teacher.

One reason for accepting control from teachers in other lessons, from the pupils' point of view, is because they lead to examination results which in turn lead to jobs.

> People would concentrate on PSE if there was an exam at the end. I don't want one, because that'd be another exam, but if people thought they had to work towards something they would concentrate.

> There would be a reason to listen.

> But we haven't got anything, we don't get a grade, or an exam that would help us, or anything. So there's nothing to work for.
>
> (School A)

If teachers ask pupils to discuss issues or themes in PSE time which lacks all the main recognition rules available in all other curriculum areas, pupils often fail to see the point of it and it is hardly surprising that they tend to associate the range of legitimate meanings with the idiosyncracies and moral preferences of individual teachers. Some pupils, especially those in academic groups, were quite cynical of teachers' motives for teaching PSE:

> It's so they can say, 'Oh they know it. We've told them. So, if they go away and abuse alcohol, it's their fault 'cos we've told them about how evil it is so, it's their fault. So, we've covered ourselves.'
>
> (School A)

A different conception of quality in PSE is clearly going to be needed if it is going to compensate for the deficiencies we have identified in the permeation approach to the teaching of themes and provide opportunities for pupils of all social backgrounds to have access to the range of meanings needed for genuine empowerment in the world beyond school.

Assessing the Themes

Meanwhile, many people still expect the themes to fulfil the requirements of Section One of the Reform Act, with the implication that themes can affect the lives of pupils outside school in a way that subjects do not. In the light of our findings, there is clearly an urgent need to rethink cross-curricular provision and to provide more appropriate recognition and realisation rules.

Bernstein (1971) identifies evaluation (or assessment) as a third 'message system' operating in schools alongside – and often driving – curriculum and pedagogy. The evaluation message system in schools is provided mainly through the examination system and the lack of a distinctive assessment system for the themes helps to explain their lack of visibility and status. So far, little attention seems to have been given to this in discussions about the themes. Where themes are delivered exclusively through subjects, the components are likely to be assessed in relationship to the attainment targets for particular subjects rather than in terms of their relationships to other subjects or to pupils' life outside schools. Yet, if subject discourses are aimed at transmitting abstract principles then the forms of assessment used for subjects will not be entirely appropriate to themes.

Alternative modes of assessment could help to provide appropriate recognition and realisation rules for the themes and/or for PSE. Ideally, this would demand that pupils pull together appropriate knowledge from a range of subjects, and the criteria for successful learning in relation to the themes would thus need to be based on the ability of pupils to integrate knowledge. Some may wish to go further and suggest that the assessment of such knowledge should be tied to social issues which are relevant to pupils' lives or even to social behaviour. In this case, the assessment procedures for themes would be most unlikely to involve standard paper and pencil testing. In our survey, though, 63 per cent of schools had no plans to assess themes separately from subjects. Of the 37 per cent of schools that stated that they did intend to assess the themes separately from subjects, a few felt it important to give themes status by formally examining them in some way but most of these schools were referring to entries in pupils' Records of Achievement.

Towards the end of the project, we conducted a telephone survey followed by fieldwork in six schools that had tried to use such devices. This showed that the actual use of Records of Achievement for reporting achievements in relation to the cross-curricular themes was even more limited than our original survey had suggested. Nevertheless, the findings in those schools that were actually addressing this issue did reinforce the importance of having a message system to provide appropriate recognition and realisation rules for work relating to the themes. Those schools that were using integrated humanities GCSE schemes to examine work in PSE seemed to have made the most progress in establishing an identifable evaluation message system for the themes. This gave PSE a status that approximated to that associated with at least some of the National Curriculum subjects but employed a more flexible approach to assessment. We were also impressed by the way in which one school was using the nationally recognised Youth Awards Scheme (now ASDAN awards) to enhance the visibility and status of theme-related work without translating it into a largely academic mode. Yet another school was trying to use the Duke of Edinburgh's award scheme in this way.

Without such alternative forms of assessing and recording work related to the themes, the burden of decontextualising theme-related knowledge from subjects and recontextualising it in everyday life will have to be shouldered largely by pupils themselves. The burden might be lightened, firstly, by theme-related knowledge being highlighted in some way for pupils in subjects and, secondly, if time is provided in the curriculum where pupils can be helped to recontextualise the appropriate aspects of subject knowledge. Such changes would be greatly facilitated by new approaches to assessment in social education to replace or supplement those employed in National Curriculum subjects or in PSE in most of our fieldwork schools. Even so, given the culture of secondary school teaching and the enduring tensions between subject knowledge and everyday life, it will not be easy to gain widespread acceptance of such devices.

Conclusion

The idea of having cross-curricular themes threaded through subjects has not proved to be an effective way of dealing with curricular overload, the ambiguous status of PSE in many schools and the limitations of traditional school subjects as a basis for social education. Nevertheless, in principle, there is still considerable support for the themes or, at least, a recognition that they were partly designed to meet an important educational need. In practice, though, our research suggested that the notion of theme-related cross-curricular provision through subjects as the main strategy for social education will clearly need to be rethought in future revisions of the National Curriculum, something that has now been recognised to the extent that citizenship is to become part of statutory provision from 2002. However, the related tensions between academic and vocational education remain a key issue both in the sociology of education (Young, 1998b) and in education policy (DfEE, 2001).

Further Reading

Bernstein, Basil (1977) *Class, Codes and Control, Vol. 3*, 2nd edn. London: Routledge & Kegan Paul.

Bernstein, Basil (2000) *Pedagogy, Symbolic Control and Identity*. Revised edition. Lanham, MD: Rowman & Littlefield.

Young, Michael (1998) *The Curriculum of the Future*. London: Falmer Press.

Notes

1. In addition to the five cross-curricular 'themes', the National Curriculum Council (1990b) identified a number of cross-curricular 'skills' and 'dimensions'. This chapter focuses only on the themes.
2. This research was funded by Grant No. L20825201001 from the Economic and Social Research Council as part of a research programme on 'Innovation and Change in Education: The Quality of Teaching and Learning'. A fuller account of the research can be found in Whitty et al. (1994a, 1994b).
3. The notion of permeation here does not necessarily imply that the boundaries between subjects were permeable, merely that the teaching of the themes was distributed across a variety of separate subjects.

3

Devolution and Choice in Three Countries
with Sally Power

This chapter is concerned with the fashionable 'school autonomy' and 'parental choice' agendas that have dominated contemporary education policy in many countries in recent years. It focuses on the nature of such policies in England and Wales, the USA and New Zealand, where the neo-liberal ideas have been particularly influential. It goes on to review the initial research evidence concerning the progress and effects of these policies and considers whether some of their benefits might be maintained while avoiding the inequitable consequences that have often been associated with them to date.

In many parts of the world, there have been attempts to move away from the 'one best system' of state-funded and state-provided education. Recent reforms have sought to dismantle centralised bureaucracies and create in their place devolved systems of schooling with increased diversity in the types of schools available, together with an increased emphasis on parental choice and competition between schools (Whitty, Power and Halpin, 1998). School autonomy, as used here, refers to school self-management through some or all aspects of funding and decision-making being devolved from regional and district offices to individual schools, whether to site-based professionals, community-based school councils or a combination of both. In considering parental choice, this chapter is particularly concerned with those policies that claim to enhance opportunities for choice among state schools and those that use public funds to extend choice into the private sector.

These policies are sometimes described as 'privatisation' of the education system. Nevertheless, if we look strictly at the issue of funding or even at provision in most countries, it is difficult to argue that education has been privatised on any significant scale (Whitty and Power, 2000). In most cases, marketisation is probably a better metaphor for what has been happening or, to be even more precise, the development of *quasi*-markets' in state-funded and/or state-provided services. Most commentators see these quasi-markets in education as involving a combination of parental choice and school autonomy, together with a greater or lesser degree of public accountability and government regulation. These kinds of reforms have been evident in many mass education systems, including those discussed in this chapter. Levacic (1995) suggests that the distinguishing characteristics of a quasi-market for a public service are 'the separation of purchaser from provider and an element of user choice between providers'. She adds that a quasi-market usually remains highly regulated, with the government controlling 'such matters as entry by new providers, investment, the quality of service (as with the national curriculum) and price, which is often zero to the user' (1995: 167). The lack of a conventional cash nexus and the strength of government intervention distinguish quasi-markets from the idealised view of a 'free' market, though few contemporary markets in any field are actually free from government regulation and many of them involve some element of overt or covert subsidy.

Nevertheless, even where quasi-markets are confined to public sector providers, it is possible to argue that some aspects of marketisation contribute to privatisation in an ideological if not a strictly economic sense. These include fostering the belief that the private sector approach is superior to that traditionally adopted in the public sector; requiring public sector institutions to operate more like those in the private sector; and encouraging private (individual/family) decision-making in place of bureaucratic fiat. In other words, they define education as a private good rather than a public issue and make education decision-making a matter of consumer choice rather than citizen rights.

Advocates of quasi-markets argue that they will lead to increased diversity of provision, better and more efficient management of schools, and enhanced professionalism and school effectiveness. Some proponents, notably Moe (1994) in the USA and Pollard (1995) in the UK, have argued that such reforms will bring particular benefits for families from disadvantaged communities, who have been ill-served by more conventional arrangements. However, critics suggest that, even if they do enhance efficiency, responsiveness, choice and diversity (and even that, they say, is questionable), they will almost certainly increase inequality between schools. Before looking at some of the initial research evidence on these matters, we outline the nature of the policies pursued in the three countries under consideration.

In England, prior to the 1980s, the vast majority of children were educated in state schools maintained by democratically elected local education authorities (LEAs) which exercised political and bureaucratic control over their schools but also often provided them with considerable professional support. After the Conservative victory at the 1979 election, the Thatcher and Major governments set about trying to break the LEA monopoly of state schooling through the provisions of a series of Education Acts passed in the 1980s and early 1990s.

Although the introduction of the National Curriculum and its associated system of testing, together with the OFSTED inspection regime, can be seen as centralising measures, most of the other reforms have been designed to enhance parental choice and transfer responsibilities from LEAs to individual schools. The earliest of these was the Assisted Places Scheme which provided public funding to enable academically able children from poor homes to attend some of the country's elite private schools (see Edwards et al., 1989). It is possible to argue that the sort of privatisation entailed within the Assisted Places Scheme suppressed marketisation within the private sector by protecting private schools from the full brunt of market forces. Indeed, some of the schools that sought to join the Scheme were considered economically vulnerable and one in Wales had to close before it could admit its first assisted place holders (Whitty, Power and Edwards, 1998).

Subsequent legislation sought to create new forms of state school entirely outside the influence of LEAs, and this marketisation of the public sector may have reduced the distinctive nature of private schools and blurred the distinction between the two sectors. City Technology Colleges (CTCs) were intended to be new secondary schools for the inner city, with a curriculum emphasis on science and technology and run by independent trusts with business sponsors. The grant-maintained schools policy enabled existing state schools to 'opt out' of their LEAs after a parental ballot and run themselves with direct funding from central government. Further legislation permitted schools to change their character by varying their enrolment schemes, encouraged new types of specialist schools and made it possible for some private schools to 'opt in' to the state system.

Local Management of Schools (LMS) gave many of those schools that remained with their LEAs more control over their own budgets and day-to-day management, receiving funds determined by the number and ages of their students. Open enrolment allowed state schools to attract as many students as possible, at least up to their physical capacity, instead of being kept to lower limits or strict catchment areas in order that other schools could remain open. This was seen as the necessary corollary of per capita funding in creating a quasi-market in education. In some respects, it was a 'virtual voucher' system (Sexton, 1987), which was expected to make all schools more responsive to their clients and either become more effective or close.

Taken together these measures were widely expected to reduce the role of LEAs to a marginal and residual one, but fewer schools left their LEAs than anticipated. Even so, while claiming to have already increased diversity and choice, Conservative prime minister John Major looked forward to the day 'when all publicly funded schools will be run as free self-governing schools'. He believed in 'trusting headmasters [sic], teachers and governing bodies to run their schools and in trusting parents to make the right choice for their children' (*The Times*, August 1994, p.5). However, his government was defeated by Tony Blair's New Labour Party in a

General Election in May 1997. Yet, although it has abolished the Assisted Places Scheme, the new government has maintained most of the key features of the Conservative government's approach, and has actually expanded its specialist school programme, while introducing more central government regulation of both schools and LEAs, especially where they are seen to be failing. In the words of its leading education advisor, New Labour has sought to link 'its traditional concern with equality with a new recognition of diversity' (Barber, 1997a: 175).

By contrast with England, New Zealand in the 1980s was a somewhat surprising context for a radical experiment in school reform, let alone one associated with a conservative agenda. Unlike in England and the USA, there was no widespread disquiet about educational standards in the state school system nor were there the vast discrepancies in school performance that contributed to a 'moral panic' about urban education in those two countries. The initial reforms were introduced by a Labour government, albeit one that had enthusiastically embraced monetarism and 'new public management' techniques, following the Picot Report of 1988 (Wylie, 1995). The education reforms, introduced in October 1989, led to a shift in the responsibility for budget allocation, staff employment and educational outcomes from central government and regional educational boards to individual schools. Schools were given boards of trustees that have effective control over their enrolment schemes, with even lighter regulation than in England.

However, Wylie argues that other aspects of the New Zealand reforms 'offer a model of school self-management which is more balanced than the English experience'. This is because they put 'a great emphasis on equity...on community involvement...on parental involvement [and on] partnership: between parents and professionals' (1994: xv). Furthermore, neither the costs of teacher salaries nor of some central support services were devolved to individual school budgets, though there were subsequently moves in this direction after the election of a National Party administration in 1990. Only 3 per cent of New Zealand schools were in a pilot scheme for 'bulk funding' (or devolution of 100 per cent of their funding including teachers' salaries), but a 'full funding' option was opened up to all schools in 1996 for a trial period of three years and had attracted 20 per cent of schools by 1998 (Wylie, 1998a). Unlike the original English funding formulae, which funded schools on the basis of average teacher salaries, the New Zealand scheme was based on actual teacher salaries and a given teacher:student ratio. Alongside these reforms, national curriculum guidelines were introduced but these were far less detailed and prescriptive than the English model and paid more attention to minority Maori interests. However, an ambitious outcome-based national assessment system was introduced, as was a new approach to inspection by the Education Review Office. The extension of choice into the private sector began in 1996 with a New Zealand equivalent of the Assisted Places Scheme, called Targeted Individual Entitlement, involving about a third of private schools, leading to claims that it marked 'the start of a move towards a voucher system in which schools compete for parents' education dollar' (*Wellington Evening Post*, 28 September 1995). By 1999, Wylie (1999a) suggested that, taken together, New Zealand policies now added up to a 'quasi-voucher system'. However, a Labour/Alliance party coalition then replaced the conservative National party in government and, during 2000, it significantly constrained market forces by bringing in new admissions rules, abolishing Targeted Individual Entitlement and ending the bulk funding of teachers' salaries. At the same time, it has introduced target-setting and intervention in failing schools along similar lines to the re-regulation brought in by New Labour in England.

In the USA, the limited role of the federal government in relation to education makes it harder to generalise about the nature and provenance of policies designed to enhance parental choice and devolve decision-making to schools. The more significant decisions are taken at state and district levels. While a few states, such as Minnesota, have state-wide choice plans, many initiatives have been more local. Wells (1993b) demonstrates the huge variety in origins and likely effects of the various choice plans that have been mooted or implemented in the US over the past few years. Similarly, American specialist or 'focus' schools have very different origins and purposes (Raywid, 1994; Hill, Foster and Gendler, 1990). They include long-standing specialty schools, such as the Boston Latin School and New York's highly academic Stuyvesant High School, magnet schools associated with desegregation plans, alternative schools, sometimes based on progressive pedagogic principles, and private Catholic schools. The nature of the more recent wave of semi-autonomous charter schools that have developed in many states and that of site-based management within school districts also varies considerably (Wohlstetter et al., 1995; Wells et al., 1999; Johnson and Landman, 2000). A variety of programmes to enable low-income families to choose private schools have also become a feature of urban education in the USA. In addition to the two controversial publicly funded schemes in Milwaukee and Cleveland, over 30 cities now have privately funded schemes (Peterson, 1998).

Devolution and choice in the USA enlists significant support from progressive forces, particularly amongst those representing minority ethnic groups. The mixed evidence about the efficacy and effects of desegregation and magnet schools in the 1980s (Blank, 1990; Moore and Davenport, 1990) has sometimes led to the conclusion that enhanced parental voice and choice, rather than more concerted political intervention, will provide the best chance of educational salvation for minority parents and their children. Moe (1994) went so far as to claim that the best hope for the poor to gain the right 'to leave bad schools and seek out good ones' was through an 'unorthodox alliance' with 'Republicans and business...who are the only powerful groups willing to transform the system' (1994: 33). For this reason, some aspects of the current reform agenda have developed a populist appeal well beyond the coteries of conservative politicians or even the white populations to which they usually appeal. Goldhaber (1999) reported that, for the first time, a plurality of survey respondents favoured the use of vouchers for private school tuition (Rose and Gallup, 1999) and it is likely that the Bush government will encourage more experiments of this type.

In so far as it is possible to generalise, then, the New Zealand reforms ushered in a more thorough-going experiment in free parental choice in the state sector than has been tried in England, while both these countries have gone further in this respect than all but a few school districts in the USA. In terms of freedom from local bureaucratic control, New Zealand schools have the most autonomy and those in the USA the least. Within England, grant-maintained schools (now renamed 'foundation schools' by the New Labour government) have the most autonomy, but even mainstream LEA schools, which virtually all now have local management, have considerably more autonomy than most US schools even after the re-regulation introduced by New Labour. As for freedom in financial management, English schools operating under LMS or Labour's new 'fair funding' regime have more resources under their direct control than even New Zealand schools, apart from those of the latter which participated in the 'full funding' trials. In the USA, financial devolution within school districts has not gone nearly as far as it has in either England or New Zealand. In that respect, little of the American experience of site-based management is directly relevant to the claims made by advocates of more radical supply side reforms. What may be instructive, though, is the increasing use of for-profit companies in the running of public schools. Within the UK this is a relatively recent phenomenon and currently there are only a handful of 'privately run' publicly funded schools and LEAs – although more are envisaged. In the USA, though, for-profit companies are the fastest growing sector of the charter school movement (Ascher and Power, 2000). An additional development in the States which may become more widespread is the growth of 'homeschooling' (Apple, 2001) – perhaps an example of privatisation in its most literal sense.

Finally, equity considerations have had different degrees of influence in the three countries. For example, 'race' has been a much more influential issue in the USA and New Zealand than it has so far in England where a government minister once dismissed concerns about the possibility of racial segregation with the statement that her government did not wish 'to circumscribe [parental] choice in any way' (quoted in Blackburne, 1988). It has influenced policies in New Zealand (in terms of funding and community influence) and in the USA (in relation to funding and enrolment policies) far more than it has in England. Thus, in a number of US states, charter law included provisions stipulating that charter schools reflect the racial balance in the surrounding district, or that these schools give priority to 'at risk' students.

We now consider the limited evidence that is available about the effects of these recent policies to encourage parental choice and school self-management in these three countries.

Research on the Effects of Reform

In England and Wales, there is nothing to suggest that any gains have been substantial even in relation to the claims that the reforms would lead to more effective use of resources.   A national study conducted by Birmingham University and funded by the National Association of Head Teachers was generally positive about the impact of LMS but conceded that direct evidence of the influence of self-management on learning was 'elusive'. The team's initial survey (Arnott et al., 1992) showed that the vast majority of headteachers agreed with the statement that 'local management allows schools to make more effective use of its resources'. However, a majority also felt that meetings were being taken up by administrative issues which lessened their attention to students' learning. They were thoroughly divided on the question of whether 'children's learning is benefiting from local management'. Thus it was rather unclear what their concept of greater effectiveness actually related to.

The results cited here came mainly from headteacher respondents, whose authority has been greatly enhanced by the self-management reform. It may be significant that the relatively few classroom teachers who were interviewed by the Birmingham research team were far more cautious about the benefits of LMS for student learning and overall standards. An independently funded study (Levacic, 1995) found headteachers generally welcomed self-management even where their school had lost resources as a result of it, while classroom teachers were sceptical about its benefits even in schools which had gained in resources. Levacic concludes that, although local management enhances cost-efficiency, there is 'a lack of strong theoretical argument and empirical evidence' to show that it improves the quality of teaching and learning, as claimed by the government (Levacic, 1995: xi).

In later reports of the Birmingham study (Bullock and Thomas, 1994, 1997), relatively more headteachers claimed improvements in student learning, but significantly these seem to be associated with increased funding rather than self-management per se. While the Birmingham team concluded that self-management was broadly a successful reform, they argued that more evidence was needed on the relationship between resourcing levels and learning outcomes. This seems particularly important in that the schools most affected by budgetary difficulties, and therefore least likely to report a positive impact on students' learning, were often found to be those with students from disadvantaged backgrounds.

The Birmingham study echoes some of the concerns expressed by Le Grand and Bartlett (1993) in their study of quasi-markets in social policy. Bartlett (1993) points out that, although parental choice has been increased by open enrolment, 'the door is firmly closed once a school [is full]. And by encouraging an increasingly selective admissions policy in [over-subscribed] schools open enrolment may have the effect of bringing about increased opportunities for cream-skimming and hence inequality.' Furthermore, he found that 'those schools which faced financial losses under the formula funding system tended to be schools which drew the greatest proportion of students from the most disadvantaged section of the community' (Bartlett, 1993). Thus whatever gains may have emerged from the reforms in terms of efficiency and responsiveness to some clients, there were serious concerns about their implications for equity.

The danger of 'cream skimming' is clearly demonstrated in an important series of studies by Ball and his colleagues on the operation of quasi-markets in London. In an early study, Bowe et al. (1992) suggested that schools were competing to attract greater cultural capital and thus hoping for higher yielding returns. Subsequently, Gewirtz et al. (1995) have shown schools seeking students who are 'able', 'gifted', 'motivated and committed', and middle class, with girls and children with South Asian backgrounds being seen as particular assets in terms of their potential to enhance test scores. The least desirable clientele include those who are 'less able', have special educational needs, especially emotional and behavioural difficulties, as well as children from working-class backgrounds and boys, unless they also have some of the more desirable attributes.

There is certainly evidence that some schools discriminate against children with special educational needs (Feintuck, 1994). Bartlett (1993) argues that only if the market price varies with the needs of the client will this not happen. In other words, funding formulae need to be weighted to give schools an incentive to take more expensive children. The current premium paid for children with special educational needs may not be enough, if it makes the school less popular with clients who, although bringing in less money, bring in other desirable attributes. Bowe et al. (1992) and Vincent et al. (1995) give examples of schools making just this sort of calculation.

The academically able are the 'cream' that most schools seek to attract. Such students stay in the system longer and thus bring in more money overall, as well as making the school appear successful in terms of its test scores and hence attractive to other desirable clients. Glennerster (1991) suggests that, given the opportunity, most schools will want to become more selective because taking children who will bring scores down will affect their overall market position. This is especially so when there is imperfect information about school effectiveness and when only 'raw' test scores are made available as they have been hitherto in England. Schools with the highest scores appear best even if other schools enhance achievement more.

Partly because of this ranking system on a unidimensional scale of academic excellence, there is little evidence that choice policies are fostering horizontal diversity in schooling. Glatter et al. (1997) found no evidence of greater diversity of provision, except where there was specific government funding for specialist schools. In some cases, they identified a tendency towards greater uniformity between schools. Some commentators have even predicted that, rather than choice leading to more diverse and responsive forms of provision as claimed by many of its advocates, it will reinforce the existing hierarchy of schools based on academic test results and social class (Walford and Miller, 1991).

Those parents who are in a position to choose are choosing those schools that are closest to the traditional academic model of education that used to be associated with selective grammar schools. Even new types of school tend to be judged in these terms. Our research showed many parents choosing CTCs not so much for their 'high tech' image, but because they were perceived as the next best thing to grammar schools or even elite private schools (Whitty et al., 1993). In this situation, those *schools* that are in a position to choose often seek to identify their success with an emphasis on traditional academic virtues and thus attract those students most likely to display them. Many of the first schools to opt out and become grant maintained were selective, single sex and with traditional sixth forms and this gave the sector an aura of elite status (Fitz et al., 1993). Some grant-maintained comprehensive schools subsequently reverted to being overtly academically selective, and Bush et al. (1993) suggested that 30 per cent of the grant maintained 'comprehensive' schools they investigated were using covert selection. In addition, grant-maintained schools were identified as among those with the highest rates of exclusion of existing students and among the least willing to cater for students with special educational needs (Feintuck, 1994). Recent research by Levacic and Hardman (1999) also reveals that the examination results of these schools rose as the proportion of socio-economically disadvantaged children within them declined. To that extent they can hardly claim to have increased parental choice and pupil performance across the board (Power et al., 1994).

Walford argues that, while choice will lead to better quality schooling for some children, the evidence so far suggests that it will 'discriminate in particular against working-class children and children of Afro-Caribbean descent' (1992: 137). Smith and Noble (1995) also conclude from the evidence that English choice policies are further disadvantaging already disadvantaged groups. Although schools have always been socially and racially segregated to the extent that residential segregation exists, Gewirtz et al. (1995) suggest that choice may well exacerbate this segregation by extending it into previously integrated schools serving mixed localities. Their research indicates that working-class children and particularly children with special educational needs are likely to be increasingly 'ghettoised' in poorly resourced schools.

Although it is argued that schemes such as the Assisted Places Scheme allow able and meritorious working-class children to 'escape' from such schools, they have been shown to attract relatively few children from such backgrounds (Edwards et al. 1989). Furthermore, the existence of such escape routes reduces the pressure to improve the schools in which the majority of working-class children continue to be educated, thus potentially increasing the overall polarisation of standards of provision. The Smithfield Project, a major government-funded study of the impact of choice policies in New Zealand (Lauder et al., 1994; Waslander and Thrupp, 1995; Lauder et al., 1999) has suggested that much the same sort of social polarisation is taking place there. Although Gorard and Fitz (1998a) have questioned this particular analysis, other New Zealand studies have provided evidence of similar effects (Nash and Harker, 1998). In another study (Fowler, 1993), schools located in low socio-economic areas were found to be judged negatively because of factors over which they had no influence, such as type of intake, location and problems perceived by parents as linked to these. Wylie (1994) too noted that schools in low income areas there are more likely to be losing students to other schools. If we could be sure that their poor reputation was deserved, this might be taken as evidence that the market was working well with effective schools reaping their just rewards. But, as in England, judgements of schools tend to be made on social grounds or narrow academic criteria and with little reference to their overall performance or even their academic effectiveness on value-added measures. The funding regime makes it extremely difficult for schools in disadvantaged areas to break out of the cycle of decline and this exacerbates the problems facing teachers and students remaining in them. Wylie's study of the fifth year of self-managing schools in New Zealand (Wylie, 1994) identified schools in low income areas, and schools with high Maori enrolments, as experiencing greater resource problems than others.

Wylie (1994, 1995) reported that quasi-markets had led to state schools paying more attention to the attractiveness of physical plant and public image than to changes in teaching and learning other than the spread of computers. Even by the seventh year study in 1996, only 34 per cent of primary school principals and 24 per cent of teachers thought the reforms had had 'a major positive impact on the quality of children's learning in school' (Wylie, 1997). As in England, schools that had increasing or stable rolls (and funding) were much more likely to report positive impacts than those that were losing students. And, again, schools with low socio-economic status intakes were more likely to have lost out and, significantly, there had been a slight decline in Maori student achievement in the period since the reforms were introduced (Wylie, 1998a).

Wylie has noted that the reforms 'do not seem able to counter or outweigh factors affecting school rolls which lie beyond school power, such as local demographics affected by employment, ethnicity, and class' (Wylie, 1995, citing Gordon, 1994; Waslander and Thrupp, 1995). The lack of any marked improvement in overall standards and the continued existence of socially-patterned achievement gaps have led her to argue that placing school self-management at the centre of educational reform is unlikely to bring significant gains in effectiveness in the absence of other changes (Wylie, 1998a). Furthermore, there seems to be little to suggest that market mechanisms are the key, either to the improvement of failing schools or to enhanced achievement for disadvantaged students (Fiske and Ladd, 2000). Schools which were most positive about the reforms were those that had 'co-operative rather than competitive relations with other schools' (Wylie, 1997: 1). Policies of enhancing what Wylie terms 'family choice' have 'done little to substantially improve access to more desirable schools for Maori or low-income students' (Wylie, 1999b: 13). In a 1999 survey, they were found to be significantly less likely to have received their first choice of school than other students. Nor have the policies improved conditions at the schools most such students actually attend. Indeed, she concludes 'the policies appear to have made things somewhat worse for the very group intended to benefit most from them' (Wylie, 1999b: 13). Wylie (1998b) also cites an evaluation by Smith and Gaffney (1997) as showing that, although the Targeted Individual Entitlement Scheme to give private school places to low income families was somewhat better targeted than its English equivalent, it attracted relatively fewer Maori and Pacific Island children than those from other low income groups.

Overall, this work suggests that many of the differences between schools result from factors largely beyond the control of parents and schools, except the power of advantaged parents and advantaged schools to further enhance their advantage and thus increase educational inequalities and social polarisation. This does not necessarily mean that devolution and choice will need to be entirely abandoned in New Zealand, but it is clear that they need to be accompanied by other policies. As in England, the weaknesses of the policies have already produced a degree of re-regulation on the part of central government, but under the

National government this took the form of tightened inspection and technical control through more prescriptive curriculum and assessment policies which have been only marginally modified by the Labour/Alliance government (Wylie, 1998a; D. McKenzie, 1999). However, the new government does seem to have taken some note of the research that points to a need for far more support for disadvantaged schools and concerted collaboration between government and schools rather than the current segmentation of responsibility. Furthermore, procedures for selection to oversubscribed schools have been revised. Significantly, the Smithfield Project had found that, only in one year where allocations to oversubscribed schools were based on 'balloting' (or drawing lots), did social polarisation between popular and unpopular schools decrease and this has influenced the new regulations.

As indicated above, some of this research has been challenged by Gorard and Fitz (1998a, 1998b) who have claimed that the tendency towards increased polarisation in both England and Wales and New Zealand may have been merely an initial effect of marketisation policies and that social polarisation has actually been reduced in subsequent years. However, Noden (2000) has argued that his own more robust methodology paints a less positive picture. Using an index of isolation, rather than the index of dissimilarity employed by Gorard and Fitz, Noden claims that between 1994 and 1999 English secondary schools experienced a significant increase in socio-economic segregation. Gorard and Fitz themselves have since reported that some recent statistics show evidence of renewed social polarisation, but their overall position seems to be that 'the advent of choice may be truly both less beneficial than some advocates suggest, and less harmful than some critics fear' (Cassidy, 2000). Meanwhile, educational polarisation has been confirmed in the case of England by Her Majesty's Chief Inspector of Schools (HMCI, 1998) and the 1998 GCSE public examination results brought an increase in the failure rate alongside an increase in the numbers gaining high grade passes. On the other hand, the most recent government statistics suggest that the achievement gap is now being narrowed for some, though not all, minority ethnic groups.

In the USA, despite the early association of public school choice with racial desegregation, there are considerable concerns about the equity effects of more recent attempts to enhance choice, especially as there is no clear evidence to date of a positive impact on student achievement. What evidence there is about the effects of choice policies on student achievement and equity continues to be at best inconclusive (Plank et al., 1993), notwithstanding claims by choice advocates that 'the best available evidence' shows that parental choice improves the education of all children, especially low income and minority students' (Domanico, 1990).

Even some of the more positive evidence from controlled choice districts, such as Cambridge (Rossell and Glenn, 1988) and Montclair (Clewell and Joy, 1990), which seemed to show gradual overall achievement gains, has subsequently been regarded as methodologically flawed (Henig, 1994) making it difficult to attribute improvements to choice per se. Furthermore, although choice has not always led to resegregation as its critics feared, improvements in the racial balance of Montclair and Cambridge schools were most noticeable during periods of strong government intervention. Henig goes on to argue that the much vaunted East Harlem 'miracle' (Fliegel, 1990) has 'escaped any serious effort at controlled analysis' even though it has had a special role 'in countering charges that the benefits of choice programs will not accrue to minorities and the poor' (1990: 142). Not only have the apparently impressive gains in achievement now levelled off or even been reversed, it is impossible to be sure that the earlier figures were not merely the effect of schools being able to choose students from higher socio-economic groups from outside the area. There are certainly grounds for suggesting that current public choice programmes will eventually lead to increasing segregation of schools. In a recent review of the American research, Goldhaber (1999: 21) argues that 'existing empirical evidence on "who chooses" generally shows choice (in any of its forms) to be highly correlated with SES'. His own research (Goldhaber, 1996) also points to a racial dimension in that parents tend to prefer schools with a higher proportion of white students.

Research on the effects of school autonomy in the US is also inconclusive, not least because the degree of autonomy granted to mainstream public schools with site-based management is, as we have seen, substantially lower than in England or New Zealand. As for the growing number of publicly funded charter schools, Goldhaber (1999) argues that it is too early to undertake quantitative assessments of their impact and points out that most claims of success tend to be based on anecdote. However, while there is little to suggest these schools have been particularly mould-breaking, neither have they become the elite institutions many feared (OERI, 1997).

The American evidence with regard to private school choice is contentious, but highly relevant to our concerns in view of current demands for an extension of the use of public funds to permit students to attend private schools. Much of the controversy centres around the various interpretations of the data from Coleman's high school studies (Coleman et al., 1982) and, in particular, the work of Chubb and Moe (1990). Henig (1994) argues that the small advantage attributed to private schools is a product of the methodology used. Lee and Bryk (1993) also suggest Chubb and Moe's conclusions are not supported by the evidence as presented. Nevertheless, Bryk et al. (1993) claim on the basis of their *own* work that private Catholic schools do impact positively on the performance of low income families but they attribute this at least as much to an ethos of strong community values antithetical to the marketplace as to the espousal of market forces. Witte's evaluation of the Milwaukee 'voucher' scheme mentioned earlier, which enables children from poor families to choose private schools at public expense, concluded that 'in terms of achievement scores...students perform approximately the same as M[ilwaukee] P[ublic] S[chool] students'. However, attendance of choice children has been slightly higher and parental satisfaction has been high. For the schools, 'the program has generally been positive, has allowed several to survive, several to expand, and contributed to the building of a new school' (Witte at al., 1994). Yet neither Witte's own conclusions nor Greene and his colleagues' rather more positive reworking of the data (Greene and Peterson, 1996; Greene et al., 1998) can be used to sustain some of the more extravagant claims made both for and against this type of programme. It is a small and narrowly targeted programme and certainly not, of itself, a sufficient basis upon which to judge the likely effects of a more thorough-going voucher initiative.

The Milwaukee programme overall was not initially oversubscribed and, although students were self-selected, the schools involved were not generally in a position to exercise choice. Elsewhere, the combination of oversubscription and self-selection in explaining apparent performance gains through private school choice suggest that equity is a major issue as it is in England and New Zealand. Smith and Meier (1995) used existing data to test the school choice hypothesis and concluded that 'competition between public and private schools appeared to result in a cream skimming effect' and that there was no reason to expect that the same would not happen with enhanced public school choice.

Overall, this review of the research evidence seems to suggest that the benefits of the reforms have so far been limited and that their costs, particularly for some disadvantaged groups, may have been considerable. The extravagant claims of the proponents of reform about its potential system-wide benefits have certainly not so far been realised. In making this claim, we are, of course, generalising from the evidence available. There can be no doubt that some individual disadvantaged children have benefited from the reforms. There are also instances where reforms to public education systems have made a positive difference to the educational experiences of whole groups of students and teachers. The Kura Kaupapa Maori in New Zealand and some of the 'alternative' US charter schools provide examples where self-determination by communities and professionals has brought about innovative and potentially empowering educational environments. However, there are doubts as to the sustainability of such programmes and about the extent to which they can be attributed to quasi-markets rather than to other changes (Thrupp, 1999). Moreover, these innovative instances need to be set alongside a prevailing pattern of educational conservatism and consolidated hierarchies both within and between schools.

Beyond Quasi-Markets?

Advocates of market forces have argued that the indifferent performance of the reforms so far is merely evidence that they have not gone far enough. Thus, some commentators from the radical right see the answer as moving still further towards more genuinely marketised and even fully privatised forms of education provision. For example, a government Minister responsible for the introduction of the Assisted Places Scheme in England used our own research (Edwards et al., 1989) showing that it had failed to attract many working-class students as a basis for arguing in favour of a fully-fledged voucher scheme (Boyson, 1990). Similarly, Moe's (1994) only major criticism of the British reforms was that the Conservative government had 'created an open enrolment system in which there is very little to choose from, because the supply of schools is controlled by the LEAs'. In order to free up the supply side, he suggested that all schools should become autonomous. Tooley (1996) favours an even more deregulated system and the abandonment of a centrally prescribed curriculum. To the architect of New Zealand's neoliberal reforms it is also a case of 'unfinished business' (Douglas, 1993).

Much of the support for moving further towards decentralising education provision derives from the alleged benefits of private provision. As we discussed earlier, the evidence with regard to existing schemes of private school choice is contentious. In discussing the US experience, Wylie argues that 'it is difficult to keep voucher schemes limited to low income or minority groups' (1998b: 57). It is therefore important to try to model the effects of wider schemes. Even if we accept that some children who currently attend state schools might benefit from private education, there is little to suggest that extending opportunities to attend private schools more widely would benefit all groups equally. Witte at al. (1995) have undertaken an analysis of the current social composition of private and public schools in the American state of Wisconsin and conclude that 'an open-ended voucher scheme would clearly benefit households that are more affluent than the average household in Wisconsin'. They go on to say that, although some might believe that making vouchers available to everyone would open up private schools to the poor, the opposite argument seems equally plausible. With more money available, private schools that cannot currently afford to select, such as some of the inner city private schools in the Milwaukee choice experiment, could become more selective. The already highly selective schools could then maintain their advantage by demanding add-on payments in addition to vouchers. Although this could potentially be prevented by increased regulation, even limited regulation of both selection and fee levels in connection with existing schemes has been unpopular with the private school lobby in all three countries.

Some on the right argue that these difficulties are inevitable in a system that is only partly privatised. Tooley (1995) claims that the potential of markets in education cannot be properly assessed by looking at the effects of quasi-markets, or what he prefers to term 'so-called' markets. In his own vision of *Education without the State* (Tooley, 1996) he argues that we need a 'one tier private system' and that parents and students should be free to determine the kind of schooling they feel suits them best. He envisages lowering the school leaving age and providing every student with a 'lifelong individual fund for education' which they would then be able to spend when amd where they saw fit. Tooley is right to remind us of the shortcomings of existing democratic systems and, of course, research on current systems does not, indeed in principle could not, show that total deregulation would not have beneficial effects. Yet, most of the available evidence does seem to suggest that going further in the direction of marketisation and privatisation would be unlikely to yield overall improvements in the quality of education and might well have damaging equity effects. Recently, Tooley (2000) has criticised our book (Whitty, Power and Halpin, 1998), partly because he does not entirely believe the evidence we cite, but mainly because it relates to a situation where markets are not fully deregulated in the manner he favours.

Yet, even Chubb and Moe (1990), who argue that equality is better 'protected' by markets than political institutions, concede that choice of school in a democracy cannot be unlimited or entirely unregulated. The need to provide a balance between consumer rights and citizen rights in education, while recognising the desirability of some facets of choice and devolution, has already led in England to proposals to put a greater degree of democratic control back in the picture. In particular, there has been discussion around how to revive democratic involvement and account-ability at local level as a counter-balance to the market and the strong central state. For example, Pryke (1996) remarks that, 'despite the experiments to let schools do their own thing' – and he believes this has gone further in England than anywhere else in the world – 'the great majority of them, and parents, have recognised the need for a body to act for them as a community of schools' (1996: 21). Similarly, Brighouse (1996), Birmingham's senior education officer, who argues that an atomised market will create chaos and 'put further distance between the educational and social haves and the educational and social have-nots', says that 'there needs to be a local agency aware of school differences, sensitively working with each school, securing equity and setting a climate for a drive towards ever higher standards' (1996: 11). Responding to the question as to why such bodies should be democratically accountable, he suggests that in matters of education provision 'there is a need to balance various and sometimes conflicting needs and priorities [including] the needs of very different communities within, for example, a modern city' and that difference and equity can best be seen to be held in balance in an openly democratic forum (1996: 14).

Part of the challenge for those adopting this view must be to move away from atomised decision-making to the reassertion of collective responsibility without recreating the very bureaucratic systems whose shortcomings have helped to legitimate the tendency to treat education as a private good rather than a public responsibility. We need to ask how we can use the positive aspects of choice and autonomy to facilitate the development of new forms of community empowerment rather than exacerbating social differentiation. Even some reform proposals that may seem superficially to have similarities with neoliberal policies of market-isation and privatisation (e.g. Cookson, 1994; Atkinson, 1997) could become articulated with a rather different political agenda and potentially make a positive contribution to the enhancement of social justice in education.

In this context, it may well be possible to identify progressive moments within policies that foster devolution and choice. This potential was recognised in some of the early moves towards devolution in New Zealand, but the subsequent evidence suggests that it is difficult to realise progressive moments at school site level in a situation of diminishing resources and when the broader political climate is pointing in the opposite direction. Atomised decision-making in a highly stratified society may appear to give everyone equal opportunities, but transferring responsibility for decision-making from the public to the private sphere can actually reduce the possibility of collective action to improve the quality of education for all. Thus while some forms of devolution and choice may warrant further exploration as ways of realising the legitimate aspirations of disadvantaged groups, they are unlikely to be able to counteract the effects of wider structural inequalities on a sustained and consistent basis. Lauder et al. (1998) have argued for a 'contextual model' for research on school effectiveness which, while recognising that individual schools can and do sometimes make a difference, would explore the specific conditions under which school processes are or are not relatively autonomous from wider social and political processes.

Meanwhile, in seeking out ways of responding to this challenge in policy terms, many are looking to see how far the new governments in all three countries will either modify or extend neoliberal policies. Of particular interest to many international observers is the New Labour government in Britain, which has been drawing on critiques of both traditional social democratic forms and neoliberal market forms to develop a so-called 'Third Way' (Giddens, 1998). In the light of concerns about some of the negative equity effects of quasi-markets, the New Labour government promised to move beyond the 'ruthless free-for-all' of the neoliberals. As we saw in Chapter 1, rather than revisiting the 'stifling statism' of 'Old Labour', the Blair government has claimed to be developing policies on the basis of 'what works' rather than being driven by any one ideological approach. Yet it remains unclear whether the current mixture of apparently discordant strategies can succeed in delivering the claimed benefits of devolution and choice while also overcoming prevailing patterns of inequality. Tooley (2000) may well be right to raise questions about the capacity of existing policies to deliver, but his own entirely privatised free market alternative is surely not the only option left. In the next chapter, where I consider the implications for the teaching profession of the sorts of policies discussed here, I suggest that there might be more democratic alternatives to both statist and market approaches.

Further Reading

Gewirtz, Sharon, Ball, Stephen and Bowe, Richard (1995) *Markets, Choice and Equity*. Buckingham: Open University Press.

Tooley, James (2000) *Reclaiming Education*. London: Cassell.

Whitty, Geoff, Power, Sally and Halpin, David (1998) *Devolution and Choice in Education*. Buckingham: Open University Press.

4

Re-Forming Teacher Professionalism for New Times

This chapter discusses how far sociological discourse about professionalism and the state can help us to understand the contemporary condition of teachers as professionals as they experience the sorts of reforms discussed in Chapter 3. It then seeks to relate some of the concepts drawn from this discussion to developments in teacher education in England and Wales over the past decade. Finally, it speculates about the forms of teacher professionalism that might develop in the early years of the twenty-first century.

A great deal of recent policy discourse on education has blamed teachers for poor educational standards. Education reforms in countries as different as England and Nicaragua have limited the autonomy of teachers and curbed the power of teacher trade unions. Even in other countries, such as the USA, where the rhetoric of reform has put more emphasis on the empowerment of teachers, there has been an attempt to make teachers less the servants of local bureaucracies and more responsive to the demands of their clients. These attempts to reform and reposition the teaching profession are, of course, linked to other aspects of education reform, including the sorts of 'quasi-markets' in educational services that, as we saw in Chapter 3, emerged in the 1980s and 1990s.

In England, in particular, the reforms were accompanied by swingeing attacks on the integrity of the teaching profession in general and the teachers' unions in particular. The unions' traditional involvement in policy-making, and even in negotiating teachers' pay, was systematically undermined by the Thatcher and Major governments. These governments were strongly influenced by the pamphlets of New Right pressure groups, which argued the need to rid the system of a liberal educational establishment that had been behind the 'progressive collapse' of English education. This liberal establishment was seen as prey to ideology and self-interest and no longer in touch with the public. It was therefore 'time to set aside...the professional educators and the majority of organised teacher unions...[who] are primarily responsible for the present state of Britain's schools' (Hillgate Group, 1987). In what follows, I consider how far sociological concepts can help us make sense of such developments.

Sociological Perspectives on Professionalism

Sociologists in the 1950s and 1960s tried to establish what features an occupation should have in order to be termed a profession. So lists were compiled of the characteristics that any group worthy of the label 'profession' needed to have. A typical list included such items as the use of skills based on theoretical knowledge, education and training in those skills certified by examination, a code of professional conduct oriented towards the 'public good' and a powerful professional organisation (Millerson, 1964). Occupations that did not entirely meet such criteria – and these usually included teaching – were given the title 'quasi-' or 'semi-professions' (Etzioni, 1969). The attempt to gain the characteristics associated with professions was usually called 'professionalisation' – an occupational strategy sometimes termed the 'professional project'. Some aspects of teachers' professional project have been apparently successful, others less so. Some would say that, for schoolteachers, the arrival of the General Teaching Council (GTC) marks the turning point and that, after a century of striving, teaching in England has become a bona fide profession.

However, in common-sense terms, we have talked about a teaching profession in England for a long time. We have not tended to say that teachers in Scotland have been a profession, because they have had a GTC for many years, while those in England are not. And contemporary sociologists have tended to agree, arguing that their forebears were seduced by the models of medicine and the law and have therefore imposed a normative view of what it means to be a professional as *the* essential definition of a profession. Instead, they suggest that a profession is whatever people think it is at any particular time and that can vary. So the fact that we normally talk about the teaching profession means that teaching is a profession, even when we cannot tick off all those core characteristics listed earlier.

Gerard Hanlon, whose ideas I shall return to later, argues that 'professionalism is a shifting rather than a concrete phenomenon' and states baldly that 'when I discuss professionals I am talking about groups such as doctors, academics, teachers, accountants, lawyers, engineers, civil servants, etc., that is those groups commonly thought of as professional by the lay public, academics, the professionals themselves and so on' (Hanlon, 1998: 45). It may then be more productive to explore the characteristics of teaching as an occupation in the here and now, rather than asking whether it lives up to some supposed ideal. Indeed, Eliot Freidson (1983: 33), probably the dominant American sociologist of professions in recent years, argues for seeing a profession as 'an empirical entity about which there is little ground for generalising'.

This has implications for current debates about teacher professionalism in the twenty-first century. Some critics have argued that teaching is being 'de-professionalised' as a result of recent education reforms. But the proponents of the reforms might wish to characterise the process as one of 're-professionalisation', making teacher professionalism more in keeping with the needs of a new era. However, if we are standing back from our own assumptions and preferences, and adopting the stance of sociologist, it is probably best to see all these various positions as *competing* versions of teacher professionalism for the twenty-first century rather than seeing any one as fitting an essentialist definition of professionalism and others as detracting from it. The particular version different people support in practice will, of course, depend on their values and their broader political perspectives, as well as the way in which they are positioned by the reforms.

So where does the state come into this? Professional status can also depend on the sort of bargain an occupation has struck with the state – what is sometimes called its 'professional mandate'. Traditionally professions were independent and self-governing and individual professionals have often been self-employed. But in industrial societies today, most professionals are directly employed and/or regulated by the state. As Dale (1989) puts it, some professions have a licensed form of autonomy, others regulated autonomy. Medicine and law, and arguably even nursing, have to some extent been licensed to manage their own affairs. The teaching profession in England has hitherto not been formally licensed in this way, but in the 1960s teachers were seen to have a considerable degree of de facto autonomy. Indeed, Le Grand (1997) suggests that in England, during the so-called 'golden age of teacher control' from 1944 to the mid-1970s, parents of children in state schools were expected to trust the professionals and accept that teachers knew what was best for their children. The state did not seem to want to intervene, even though effectively it paid teachers' salaries.

However, a view emerged in the 1970s that teachers had abused this licensed autonomy to the detriment of their pupils and society. Public choice theorists argued that the behaviour of public servants and professionals could actually be better understood if they were assumed to be largely self-interested. Many professional groups and particularly the 'liberal educational establishment' of the 'swollen state' of postwar social democracy came to be regarded as ill-adapted to be either agents of the state or entrepreneurial service providers in a marketised civil society. All this supported the shift to 'regulated' autonomy, involving a move away from the notion that the teaching profession should have a professional mandate to act on behalf of the state in the best interests of its citizens to a view that teachers (and other professions) need to be subjected to the rigours of the market and/or greater control and surveillance on the part of the re-formed state. So, in the 1970s, we had the William Tyndale Inquiry, Jim Callaghan's Ruskin College speech, the so-called Great Debate and, in the 1980s and 1990s, Sir Keith Joseph, Kenneth Baker, John Patten and Gillian Shephard.

Under New Labour, we have something of a paradox. At one level we have even more regulation of teachers than under the Conservative government. Yet, at the same time, with the GTC, we appear to have a shift back to licensed autonomy and on a more formal basis than ever before. Or do we? We do not yet know quite what the GTC will turn out to be and, not surprisingly, most teachers probably think it has some positive and some negative features. What does seem clear is that even licensed autonomy is not what it used to be, as even the doctors (if not yet the lawyers) are finding out. This applies both to individual professionals and to the organised profession. Effectively, as Bernstein might have put it, the state's 'modality' of control has been changing, so that it can be strong even while appearing to devolve power (Gamble, 1988).

Particularly helpful in understanding this is Neave's concept of the 'evaluative state', where what matters most is not the process by which goals or targets are achieved, but the output. In the education system, as elsewhere, there has been 'a rationalisation and wholesale redistribution of functions between centre and periphery such that the centre maintains overall strategic control through fewer, but more precise, policy levers [including] the operationalisation of criteria relating to "output quality"' (Neave, 1988: 11). Rather than leading to a withering away of the state, the state withdraws 'from the murky plain of overwhelming detail, the better to take refuge in the clear and commanding heights of strategic "profiling"' (ibid.: 12)

For teachers, this involves much clearer specification of what they are expected to achieve rather than leaving it to professional judgement. But it is not entirely true that, as Neave implies, the state thereby abandons any interest in how they achieve these things. The specification of outputs itself shapes what teachers actually do, so the state uses its levers to influence what we might call the 'content' of teachers' professionalism – or what is sometimes called teachers' 'professionality'. In the days when they had to study such things as sociology of education, generations of trainee teachers used to struggle with the distinction between 'professionalism' and 'professionality', introduced into the British literature by Eric Hoyle (1974). Hoyle used the term 'professionalism' to refer to 'those strategies and rhetorics employed by members of an occupation in seeking to improve status, salary and conditions'. But he used the term 'professionality' to refer to the 'knowledge, skills and procedures employed by teachers in the process of teaching'. There are now not only struggles over professionalism in the conventional sense, but also struggles over professionality. And the state has taken a proactive part in this, both positively (in the sense of what it should consist of) and negatively (in terms of what should be discouraged if not outlawed).

What does the struggle between the teaching profession (or at least the so-called liberal educational establishment) and the state over the nature of teachers' professionality involve? Partly, it is a struggle between 'restricted' and 'extended' professionality, another distinction that Hoyle (1974) established in the literature – though what might be included under each category has probably changed somewhat since 1974. Andy Hargreaves (1994: 19) suggests that the conventional notion of professionalism is one 'which is grounded in notions of esoteric knowledge, specialist expertise and public status' and that this is being superseded by one which involves 'the exercise of discretionary judgement within conditions of unavoidable and perpetual uncertainty'. Michael Eraut (1994) similarly emphasises a whole range of 'process knowledge' that involves making judgements as the hallmark of the modern-day professional. Yet some people argue that current moves towards competence or 'standards' based training for teachers, as sponsored by the government and the Teacher Training Agency, point in entirely the opposite direction by actually reducing the amount of control and discretion open to teachers, both individually and collectively. Jones and Moore (1993) have argued that such developments serve to undermine the dominant discourse of liberal humanism within the teaching profession and replace it with one of technical rationality, while Adams and Tulasiewicz (1995) have complained that teachers are being turned into technicians rather than 'reflective professionals'.

One way of understanding this apparent contradiction might be to see it as part of the inevitable heterodoxy of 'postmodernity', though I have counselled elsewhere against exaggerating the extent to which we have moved decisively into such a condition (Whitty and Power, 1999). Perhaps the two approaches reflect the juxtaposition of what Ronald Barnett calls 'two grand readings of our modern age'. On the one hand, there is 'a proliferation of forms of knowledge and experience', on the other a 'tendency to favour forms of knowledge of a particular – instrumental and operational – kind' (Barnett, 1994: 17). Barnett himself has suggested that 'operationalism' is a 'super-dominant tendency in higher education, which is reflective of . . . wider social forces' (ibid.:18).

Segmentation of the Teaching Profession

It is also possible that different elements of the profession are developing different forms of professionalism/professionality. Indeed, the state may even be encouraging this, with some members of the profession being given more autonomy and scope for flexibility than others, but only once they have met what might be termed a 'loyalty test'.

Hanlon (1998) suggests that virtually all professions are becoming fragmented, with some members enthusiastically adopting the changing agenda of the state and corporate employers while others are resisting it. He argues that, in the period up to about 1980, most professions (and particularly those serving the welfare state in the postwar period) developed a 'social service' form of professionalism in which professional experts were trusted to work in the best interests of everyone and the resources were made available by the state to help them do so. He shows how this is being challenged by what he calls a 'commercialised professionalism' in the public as well as the private sector, which responds more to the needs of profitability and international competitiveness and therefore privileges the needs of some clients over others. Similar developments have been evident within education as a result of policies of 'marketisation' (Whitty, Power and Halpin, 1998). Gewirtz, Ball and Bowe (1995) identify two traditions on the part of education managers, which they term 'bureau-professional' (or 'welfarist') and 'new manage-rialist'. The latter relates to the 'new public management' emphasis on such things as explicit standards/measures of performance, greater emphasis on output controls, the break-up of large entities into smaller units, market-type mechanisms, the introduction of competition and a stress on professionalised 'commercial-style' management (Bottery, 1996). Codd (1996) argues that 'there is now a dominant technocratic-reductionist managerial discourse within the culture of New Zealand schools which competes with the traditional educational discourse of many teachers' (p. 11), while Sullivan (1994) has referred to the development there of a low-trust hierarchical system rather than a high-trust collegial one.

This implies that those who are prepared to 'manage' on behalf of their employers may gain enhanced status and rewards, but those pursuing the traditional welfarist agenda are no longer trusted and have to be controlled more directly. Hanlon suggests that the clash between the two traditions will ultimately lead to a split in the professional ranks. Within teaching in England, though, there is still a struggle for hegemony in a potentially united profession, but also signs of possible fracturing along various fault lines.

Blackmore (1990) has suggested that the reforms have encouraged individual rather than collective notions of teacher professionalism. Michael Barber, a key adviser to the New Labour government, suggested that 'while individual teachers might gain, their organisations might be weakened' (1996a: 189), but (although he was a former trade union official) he did not regard that as a problem. Soucek (1996: 309) perhaps gets nearer to the heart of the matter, when he suggests that the reforms have encouraged 'political individualism' and 'technical collectivism' in that individuals in a culture of competition and performativity may be held accountable for the performance of others (through team working, quality circles and contrived collegiality) while losing their collective voice, through attacks on trade unions and the ending of collective bargaining.

Pressure on teacher trade unions has certainly been intense. In New Zealand, according to Gordon and Wilson (1992), 'the government has sought to reduce the power of teachers and their unions, to erode their conditions of work, and...to cease to recognise teachers' unions in a formal way' (1992: 257). Robertson (1995) reported pressure to break the power of the teachers' unions across Australia, as unions tried to resist the intensification of labour in schools. She further suggests that the attack on unions was designed 'to minimise the power of collective forms of representation while at the same time imparting the idea of "provider capture"' (Robertson, 1996: 15), so even effective resistance acted as a two-edged sword in that it justified further attacks. Even so, research carried out by Sinclair et al. (1993) in England suggested that the Thatcher government's reforms had not entirely succeeded in breaking down the traditional power of teacher unions within the state education system. Hatcher (1994) has argued that this was subsequently demonstrated by the successful action by teachers' unions against the workload associated with National Curriculum assessments, although Barber (1996a) claims that this represented a new form of trade unionism based on tactical alliances with parents for a particular purpose.

The reforms have meanwhile exacerbated divisions within the teaching force in other ways. As a result of the English reforms, teachers have faced not only increased workloads, but also attempts to use them more flexibly to counter the effects of budget restrictions, divisive approaches to performance related pay, and the substitution of full-time, permanent, qualified and experienced staff by part-time, temporary, less qualified and less experienced and therefore less expensive alternatives (Sinclair et al., 1993).

Not surprisingly, the casualisation of labour seems to have differential effects on males and females. Blackmore (1996) suggests that, given women's position in the peripheral labour market, they are likely to be increasingly disadvantaged and exploited by restructuring reforms under way in Australia. She regards the managerialist reality, as opposed to the collaborative rhetoric, of reform as often perpetuating 'masculinist' approaches to management. Furthermore, Chapman (1988) provides evidence from a study in Victoria which suggests that, where opportunities are made available for teachers to be involved in school-based management, men tend to take advantage of them more than women.

As we saw in Chapter 3, much of the most positive English research on the response to school-based management at school level was based on questionnaires to headteacher respondents, i.e. from those whose authority has been significantly enhanced by the self-management reform. It was noticeable that classroom teachers were far more cautious than their headteachers about its benefits (Bullock and Thomas, 1994, Marren and Levacic, 1994). This may well be because, as Blackmore puts it, the self-managing school retains 'strong modernist tendencies for a top-down, executive mode of decision-making...[alongside its] "weaker" post-modern claims to decentralise and encourage diversity, community ownership, local discretion, professional autonomy and flexible decision-making' (1995: 45). And, although particular management strategies, such as flattened hierarchies and total quality management (TQM), are entering some fields of education, they are used in a context which is arguably more neo-Fordist than post-Fordist in character.

There are nevertheless significant differences in responses to reform among classroom teachers themselves. Even in the early 1990s, Mac an Ghaill (1992), for example, identified, alongside the old-style 'professionals' and 'old collectivists', a significant minority of pro-reform teachers he called the 'new entrepreneurs'. Troman (1996) distinguished between 'old professionals', who generally sought to reject new managerialist constructions of professionalism, and a larger number of 'new professionals' who complied with some of the new demands but resisted others.

The state is unlikely to be neutral even if some of the battles are actually fought out in the professional arena, although there are different elements even within the state and probably different views within the government itself. One reading of the dominant tendency in England is that the government is preparing the leading cadres of the profession for leadership in the new marketised culture of schooling, while concluding that others have to be prevented from perpetuating an outmoded social service version of professionalism even if they cannot be won to the new agenda. In these circumstances, one would expect that new teachers would be given a rather restricted version of professionalism/professionality, but also opportunities to demonstrate their potential to join the leading cadres. Those continuing teachers who, through lack of competence or will, did not pass through the performance pay threshold would be limited to a restricted and highly regulated mode of professionalism. Those who did progress satisfactorily might be given licensed autonomy and more discretion in defining the nature of their professionality. One can see in England vestiges of virtually all the developments I have referred to here, but it is not yet clear how they will play out in the coming years.

Modes of Professionalism in Teacher Education

So, if these are some of the things that sociologists say might help us understand what is happening to the teaching profession, what implications do they have for teacher education and professional development? Although I focus here on my own area of research on initial teacher education, similar questions could usefully be asked about INSET and training for headship. I draw particularly on the 'Modes of Teacher Education' (or MOTE) research (Furlong et al., 2000).[1] This entailed national surveys of all courses conducted in 1990–91 and 1995–6 and more detailed fieldwork with 50 courses. The research was undertaken against a background of rapidly changing policy from Circular 24/89, 9/92, 14/93 onwards. Since its completion in 1996, the pace of reform has not slackened – with ever more demanding forms of inspection, a national curriculum for teacher training and league tables.

The vast majority of these policy initiatives on initial teacher education were framed with the explicit or implicit aspiration of changing the nature of teacher professionalism, even though this had at times to be pursued alongside two other policy concerns that were also significant in influencing the policies actually produced – namely, the imperative of maintaining an adequate supply of well qualified entrants to the teaching profession; and the aspiration on the part of successive Secretaries of State for Education to establish greater accountability for the content and quality of initial teacher education.

Recent governments of both political hues seem to have been convinced by New Right pressure groups that teacher educators are at the heart of a liberal educational establishment, which is wedded to outdated modes of professionalism and professionality. The preferred strategy of the neoliberal marketisers has been deregulation of the profession to allow schools to go into the market and recruit graduates (or even non-graduates) without professional training and prepare them on an apprenticeship basis in schools (Lawlor, 1990). Deregulation also had some appeal to neo-conservative critics who detected a collectivist (and even crypto-Marxist) ideological bias among teacher educators in higher education. Thus, for example, an editorial in the *Spectator* argued that the removal of 'the statutory bar on state schools hiring those with no teacher training qualification...would enable head teachers to find people...who at the moment are deterred by the prospect of having to waste a year undergoing a period of Marxist indoctrination' (*Spectator*, 27 February 1993). However, neoconservatives have also been concerned with 'enemies within' the teaching profession as a whole as well as within teacher education, so they have usually supported state prescription of what trainee teachers should learn rather than just leaving it to schools.

Both the neoliberal and the neoconservative elements of the New Right seem to have had their influence but government policies have always been something of a compromise between them, as well as with other relevant (and sometimes irrelevant) interest groups. The Conservative government's introduction of new routes into teaching and the strategy of locating more and more elements of training in schools was partly (though not wholly) a reflection of neoliberal views. However, the government did not pursue a policy of total deregulation or a wholesale devolution of teacher training to the schools, despite significant moves in that direction. Instead, a combination of neoconservative concerns and a modernising push for greater international competitiveness (Hickox, 1995) brought about an attempt to shape the content of teachers' professional knowledge through the introduction of a common list of competences or standards to be required of beginning teachers, regardless of the nature of the route by which they had achieved them.

These moves gave rise to charges that the government wanted to 'deprofessionalise' teaching. Thus, for example, Stuart Maclure (1993) suggested that the downgrading of university involvement in teacher education represented an attempt to dismantle the traditional defences of teaching as a profession. Other commentators felt that basing training in particular schools could limit the development of broader perspectives on education, and that specifying a limited range of competences would encourage restricted rather than extended professionality. More charitable observers, though, argued that the government was trying to reform teacher education in order to 're-professionalise' teaching more in line with what it perceived as the needs of the twenty-first century. Indeed, some – including David Hargreaves (1994) from within the teacher education establishment – regarded school-based training as signifying that the profession of school teaching had 'come of age' and was able to take responsibility for training its own. This view was shared by some of those enthusiasts within teaching who organised school-centred initial teacher training (SCITT) schemes (Berrill, 1994).

One of the reasons why it is possible to regard the reforms in these different lights is that they appear to embody different, even contradictory, elements. Just as in education reform more generally, there seems to have been a dual strategy of devolving some responsibilities to schools at the same time as requiring more things from the centre. To some degree, schools and teachers appeared to have been 'empowered' to develop their own 'local' professionalisms. On the other hand, centrally specified competences and standards mean that local professional freedom is actually quite tightly constrained by the demands of the 'evaluative state'. Obviously, the work of the Teacher Training Agency (TTA) established in 1994 has been particularly significant here (Mahony and Hextall, 2000). Under the leadership of its first chief executive, Anthea Millett, the TTA assisted the government in the development and codification of the earlier lists of competences into a detailed set of 'standards' for the award of Qualified Teacher Status (QTS), creating a national curriculum for initial teacher education policed by OFSTED inspection. Although these proposals originated in the last years of the Major government, they were accepted and extended by the New Labour government elected in May 1997.

To some extent, such agencies of the evaluative state represent a shift away from conventional techniques of coordination and control on the part of large-scale bureaucratic state forms and their replacement by a set of 'discursive, legislative, fiscal, organisational and other resources' (Rose and Miller, 1992: 189). Yet, these apparently 'postmodern' forms not only impact upon organisational subjectivities and professional identities, they also entail some fairly direct modes of control. Furthermore, particularly under New Labour, some of the TTA's and OFSTED's activity is reminiscent of the old-style 'bureaucratic' state, rather than the 'steering at a distance' associated with the evaluative state. Indeed, some of the TTA's key functions were taken back under the direct control of the Department for Education and Employment, though others may be devolved to the GTC in the future.

One of the problems of much of the writing about New Right ideology and state projects is that it tends to be based purely on reading the discourse rather than studying the effects and resistances that constitute ideology in practice. So, in the MOTE research, we were interested in the extent to which the reforms in initial teacher education were actually bringing about changes in the prevailing view of what it meant to be a professional teacher. Landman and Ozga have suggested that, although successive government circulars have shifted power from higher education institutions to central government and its associated agencies, teacher education has remained open to 'producer capture'. They also argue that, even though there has been a shift from 'open-ended requirements . . . to the rather more technical competences' (1995: 32), there has remained 'room for constructive interpretation' (1995: 35).

The MOTE findings provide some support for this position. We looked at the extent to which the professional autonomy of teacher educators in both higher education institutions and schools was constrained by the reforms and the extent to which the government's requirements were serving to reshape the professionality of trainee teachers. Both our national surveys asked course leaders of undergraduate and postgraduate courses whether their courses were designed on the basis of a particular view of teaching. By the time of our second survey, we were particularly interested in the extent to which the existence of an official list of competences, which has often been criticised for embodying technical rationality and neglecting more reflective and critical competences, was actually changing the model of the teacher espoused by teacher educators. In 1995–6, we found that 46 per cent of courses adhered to the notion of the reflective practitioner compared with 57 per cent at the time of the previous survey in 1990–1. Meanwhile, those specifically espousing the 'competency' model had doubled, but only to 11 per cent. Thus, even if it was somewhat less dominant than it had been five years previously, 'reflective practice', rather than technical rationality, was still by far the most popular discourse of professionalism within university- and college-based (and indeed school-centred) courses.

Another question on our second national survey asked respondents to choose three words from a list which would best characterise the sort of teacher their course aimed to produce. Despite some resistance to this question, the responses beyond 'reflective', 'professional' and 'competent' were quite varied. However, it is noteworthy that some of the terms that New Right critics often associate with HEI-based teacher education – such as 'child-centred' and 'critical' – were amongst the least popular choices. Unfortunately, we did not have a similar question on the earlier survey to compare this with. So the answers could either suggest that such aspirations were never as strong as critics suggested, or a recent drift towards the more conservative interpretations of reflective practice (Zeichner and Liston, 1987) or merely a degree of politically inspired caution in responding to the question!

Despite the continuing adherence to reflective practice, the actual use of competences in course planning, implementation and assessment increased significantly between our two surveys, well beyond the 11 per cent of courses that explicitly espoused a 'competency' model. So how can the use of competences be reconciled with the continuing attachment to the reflective practitioner model? Our second survey showed that only about 8 per cent of courses restricted themselves to using the competences specified in the government circulars, while over 75 per cent had chosen to supplement the official lists with additional competences of their own. This was consistent with our fieldwork which indicated that there was little continuing objection to the idea of competences among course leaders, but only because they felt that reflective competences could be added to the official list in order to sustain a broader definition of professionality. So course leaders appeared to be able to defend extended notions of teacher professionality while still conforming to government policy.

However, Landman and Ozga (1995) suggest that 'teacher education and training is vulnerable to the combined effects of financial stringency, devolution of budgetary control to individual schools and enhanced managerialism'. Indeed, they suspect that these might succeed where prescription by circular has failed. The MOTE research suggests that, although both forms of control have certainly been in evidence, definitions of professionality more rooted in the traditions of the profession have survived alongside the newer requirements, albeit within limits largely determined by the state.

Towards a Democratic Professionalism?

Up to this point, I have tried to stand back and examine current developments in teaching and teacher education with the eye of a sociologist. In this final section of the chapter, while still drawing upon sociological insights, I venture some opinions about what might be desirable directions for teacher professionalism and professionality in the new millennium.

As far as initial teacher education is concerned, the combination of school-based training and officially specified standards seems likely to confine the common elements of teacher professionalism increasingly to an officially prescribed national curriculum for teacher education, with a variety of 'local' professionalisms at the margins. At more advanced levels, the profession as a whole may well become more differentiated and stratified. Although such developments might be characterised as having a certain 'postmodern' cachet, it seems to me that a healthy teaching profession will require continuing efforts to maintain a more broadly defined sense of common professional identity. Perhaps the GTC will be able to deliver that, though not if it merely tries to defend conventional definitions of teacher professionalism. Nor, I would argue, if it merely seeks to mimic the 'old' professionalisms of law and medicine. But any attempt to develop an alternative conception of teacher professionalism will surely require the mobilisation of broadly based political support and not just professional partnership.

This is because, in recent years, governments and the media have encouraged the development of a 'low trust' relationship between society and its teachers, while the constant attacks on teacher educators show no sign of abating. In this context, we have to take seriously some of the charges of our critics who argue that we have abused our professional mandate and pursued our own self-interest at the expense of those less powerful than ourselves – and, in so doing, sometimes inadvertently contributed to social exclusion. Furthermore, the profession itself has not always moved to enhance its wider legitimacy. The defence of the education service has too often been conducted within the assumptions of the 'old' politics of education, which involved consultation between government, employers and unions but excluded whole constituencies – notably parents and business – to whom the New Right subsequently successfully appealed (Apple, 1996). We need to ask some fundamental questions about who has a legitimate right to be involved in defining teacher professionalism and to what end.

Conservative governments have tended to see the solution to 'producer capture' as lying in a combination of state control and market forces. New Labour has increased state regulation while seeking to 'modernise' the profession and incorporate it into its own project through a new deal for teachers based on managerialist premises and performance-related pay (DfEE, 1998). At the same time, it has given the teaching profession a GTC, but its long-term role and relationship to the TTA, OFSTED and the DfEE has still to be worked out. My own fear is that battle lines will be drawn up around the GTC between defenders of a traditional professional model and a statist one.

However, are state control and professional self-governance (or some combination of the two) the only modes of accountability open to us? Perhaps it is time instead to rethink the 'professional project'. In Australia, Knight et al. (1993) have argued that there has always been a tension between the profession's claim to autonomy and a requirement that it be open to the needs and concerns of other groups in a democratic society. Thus, like Ginsburg (1997) and Apple (1996), they suggest that there is a considerable tension between the professional project as conventionally conceived and the democratic project. However, they feel that changes in modern societies may now make it possible to resolve that tension and avoid both the teaching profession's and the state's forms of closure. Thus, for them, the alternative to state control is not traditional professionalism, but a 'democratic professionalism', which seeks to demystify professional work and build alliances between teachers and excluded constituencies of students, parents and members of the community on whose behalf decisions have traditionally been made either by professions or by the state. Celia Davies (1996: 673) also identifies 'new professionalism' or a 'democratic professionalism' as relevant to a 'changed policy context and as a solution to some of the problems of professional power long identified in the academic literature'.

So, if altruism and public service remain high on our professional agenda, the next re-formation of teacher professionalism will surely need to be one in which we harness teachers' professional expertise to a new democratic project for the twenty-first century. In general terms, too little serious thinking of this type has yet been done, notwithstanding Giddens' recent espousal of a 'Third Way' that supersedes both social democracy and neoliberalism, which I noted in Chapters 1 and 3 (Giddens, 1998). Perhaps, in relation to democratic decision-making in education, the GTC might take a lead in developing new forms of association that can provide a model for future modes of governance.

Throughout the last twenty years or so, teachers and teacher educators have been understandably preoccupied with issues of short-term survival in the face of an unrelenting flow of new initiatives and inspections. It is now time to begin working with others to develop approaches that relate not only to the legitimate aspirations of the profession but also those of the wider society – and that must include those groups which have hitherto not been well-served either by the profession or by the state. At a rhetorical level at least, that concern is increasingly embraced in the thinking of the present-day unions and in some of the policy pronouncements of New Labour. But, in the light of recent history, my question would be: is either the state or the profession really likely to face up to the challenge? The answer to this question is part of a wider set of issues concerning the state and civil society that will be discussed in the next chapter.

Further Reading

Furlong, John, Barton, Len, Miles, Sheila, Whiting, Caroline and Whitty, Geoff (2000) *Teacher Education in Transition: Re-forming Professionalism?* Buckingham: Open University Press.

Hargreaves, Andy (1994) *Changing Teachers, Changing Times*. London: Cassell.

Hoyle, Eric and John, Peter (1995) *Professional Knowledge and Professional Practice*. London: Cassell.

Note

1. 'Modes of Teacher Education: Towards a Basis for Comparison' (ESRC Research Project No. R000023810) and 'Changing Modes of Professionalism? A Case Study of Teacher Education in Transition' (ESRC Project No. R000234185). The generic title of MOTE was used informally for both projects.

5

Consumer Rights versus Citizen Rights in Contemporary Education Policy

This chapter considers the broader dynamics that underlie the specific changes in education policy discussed in earlier chapters and suggests that they involve a fundamental repositioning of education in relation to the state and civil society. It goes on to explore the implications of such changes for social justice and argues that there is an urgent need to strike a better balance between consumer rights and citizen rights in education policy if existing inequalities are not to be exacerbated.

As we saw in Chapter 3, there has been a growing emphasis on market forces in state education in many parts of the world where education has hitherto been treated as a public service. Alongside, and potentially in place of, collective provision by public bodies with a responsibility to cater for the needs of the whole population, there are increasing numbers of quasi-autonomous schools with devolved budgets competing for individual clients in the marketplace. Increasingly, education is being treated as a private good rather than a public responsibility. While calling, in response to these developments, for a reassertion of citizen rights alongside consumer rights in education, I also suggest that changes in the nature of contemporary societies require the development of new conceptions of citizenship and new forms of representation through which citizen rights can be expressed. Although, as we have seen, the celebration of diversity and choice among individuals with unequal access to cultural and material resources is likely to inhibit rather than enhance their chances of emancipation, new modes of collectivism do need to be developed that pay more attention to the legitimate aspirations of individuals from all social backgrounds.

The Neoliberal Agenda

For the neoliberal politicians who dominated educational policy-making in Britain and elsewhere in the 1980s and 1990s, social affairs are best organised according to the 'general principle of consumer sovereignty', which holds that each individual is the best judge of his or her needs and wants, and of what is in their best interests. The preference for introducing market mechanisms into education, partly from a predilection for freedom of choice as a good in itself, is also grounded in the belief that competition produces improvements in the quality of services on offer which in turn enhance the wealth-producing potential of the economy, thereby bringing about gains for the least well-off as well as for the socially advantaged.

In so far as it is accepted at all that markets have losers (even victims) as well as winners, the provision of a minimum safety net rather than universal benefits is seen as the best way to protect the weak without removing incentives or creating a universal dependency culture. But it is also sometimes claimed that the market will actually enhance social justice even for the least well-off, by placing real choice in the hands of those trapped in neighbourhood comprehensives in the inner city rather than, as before, having a system where only the wealthy or the knowing could get choice of school by moving house even if they could not afford to go private. In a strictly economic sense, these quasi-market policies cannot be regarded as privatisation of the education system, but they do require public sector institutions to operate more like private sector ones and families to treat educational decisions in a similar way to other decisions about private consumption.

Such reforms have been widely criticised from the Left, because they seem to embody a commitment to creating, not a more equal society but one that is more 'acceptably' unequal. There is no aspiration towards a rough equality of educational outcomes between different social class and ethnic groups, it being argued that such a target has brought about a 'levelling down' of achievement, and has been pursued at the expense of individual freedom. To those on the Left, it seems that individual rights are being privileged at the expense of the notion of a just social order (Connell, 1993).

However, although such reforms can be seen as a typical New Right crusade to stimulate market forces at the expense of 'producer interests', that is only one way of looking at it. Part of their wider appeal lies in a declared intention to encourage the growth of different types of school, responsive to the needs of particular communities and interest groups. This argument is especially appealing when it is linked with the claim that diversity in types of schooling does not necessarily mean hierarchy and, in this context, the new policies have gained some adherents among disadvantaged groups. They also link to concepts of multiple identities and radical pluralism and can seem more attractive than unidimensional notions of comprehensive schooling and, indeed, unidimensional notions of citizenship.

Thus, the espousal of choice and diversity in education seems superficially to resonate with notions of an open, democratic society as well as with a market ideology. Put in those terms, the new policies have a potential appeal far beyond the coteries of the New Right and have to be taken seriously by those professing a commitment to social justice. The multiple accenting of recent reforms was particularly marked in the Picot Report in New Zealand (Grace, 1991; Gordon, 1992). In Britain, the reforms were always mainly associated with a New Right agenda and the ambiguities there related as much to tensions between neoliberal and neoconservative voices as to the effects of any lingering social democratic equity agenda. However, according to Roger Dale (1994), some of the tensions might also be attributed to an emergent neo-Schumpeterian agenda evident in a recent British White Paper on economic competitiveness and influenced by policies pursued in many of the economies of the Pacific Rim.

Meanwhile, the American commentators Chubb and Moe (1992), whose work was mentioned in Chapter 3, have identified the neoliberal aspects of the British approach as 'a lesson in school reform' that other countries should follow. The rhetoric of the Conservative government's 'five great themes' – quality, diversity, parental choice, school autonomy and accountability (DFE, 1992a) – is already familiar in many other countries with different political regimes (Whitty and Edwards, 1998; Whitty, Power and Halpin, 1998). Such policies have so far been most marked in the Anglophone world, especially Britain, the USA, New Zealand and parts of Australia, but there is some evidence that their appeal has been spreading. Despite popular resistance to increased state aid to private schools in France, there has been a growing interest in deregulating schooling in various European countries. A paper by Manfred Weiss (1993) suggested that 'pluralism, decentralisation, deregulation, greater diversity and parent empowerment' were being mooted as new guiding principles in education policy in corporatist Germany. Even Taiwan, one of the 'tiger economies' of the Pacific Rim which hitherto has had a highly directed and centralist education system, has made some tentative moves in the same direction, while parts of Japan are now experimenting with school choice (Green, 2001).

Making Sense of the Reforms

In the final chapter of our book on *Specialisation and Choice in Urban Education* (Whitty et al., 1993), Tony Edwards, Sharon Gewirtz and I considered how far the British reforms might be part of a movement that is much broader and deeper than the particular set of policies that had come to be termed 'Thatcherism'. In particular, we considered how far these shifts in the nature of education policy reflected broader changes in the nature of advanced industrial societies, that is the extent to which they could be seen as a response to shifts in the economy, or more specifically patterns of production and consumption, often described as post-Fordism, and how far they might be an expression of broader social changes that are sometimes taken to signal the existence of a 'postmodern' age.

Firstly, we noted that some observers suggest that the reforms can be understood in terms of the transportation of changing modes of regulation from the sphere of production into other arenas, such as schooling and welfare services. They have pointed to a correspondence between the establishment of markets in welfare and a shift in the economy away from Fordism towards a post-Fordist mode of accumulation which 'places a lower value on mass individual and collective consumption and creates pressures for a more differentiated production and distribution of health, education, transport and housing' (Jessop et al., 1987). Various commentators, such as Stephen Ball, have claimed to see in new forms of schooling a shift from the 'Fordist' school of the era of mass production to the 'post-Fordist school' (Ball, 1990). The emergence of new and specialised sorts of school may be the educational equivalent of the rise of flexible specialisation driven by the imperatives of differentiated consumption, and taking the place of the old assembly-line world of mass production. These 'post-Fordist schools' are designed 'not only to produce the post-Fordist, multi-skilled, innovative worker but to behave in post-Fordist ways themselves; moving away from mass production and mass markets to niche markets and "flexible specialization"... a post-Fordist mind-set is thus having implications in schools for management styles, curriculum, pedagogy and assessment' (Kenway, 1993: 115). So, it is argued, the new policies not only reflect such changes, they help to foster and legitimate them.

However, we said that there were problems about assuming a straightforward correspondence between education and production, as well as with the notion of post-Fordism as an entirely new regime of accumulation. We therefore urged caution about concluding that we were experiencing a wholesale move away from a mass-produced welfare system towards a flexible, individualised and customised post-Fordist one. In the field of education, it is certainly difficult to establish a sharp distinction between mass and market systems. The so-called 'comprehensive system' in Britain was never as homogeneous as the concept of mass produced welfare suggests. Indeed, it was always a system differentiated by class and ability. We therefore felt that neo-Fordism was a more appropriate term for the recent changes than post-Fordism which implied something entirely distinctive. We suggested, however, that we might actually be witnessing an intensification of social differences and a celebration of them in a new rhetoric of legitimation. In the new rhetoric, choice, specialisation and diversity replace the previous language of common and comprehensive schooling.

Secondly, in commenting on wider changes in the nature of modern or postmodern societies, we noted that, for other commentators such as Jane Kenway, the rapid rise of the market form in education was best understood as something much more significant than post-Fordism; she therefore terms it a postmodern phenomenon (Kenway, 1993). In her pessimistic version of postmodernity, 'transnational corporations and their myriad subsidiaries...shape and reshape our individual and collective identities as we plug in...to their cultural and economic communications networks' (Kenway, 1993: 119). Her picture is one in which notions of 'difference', far from being eradicated by the 'globalization of culture', are assembled, displayed, celebrated, commodified and exploited (Robins, 1991).

But there are also other accounts of postmodernity where the rhetoric of 'new times' offers more positive images of choice and diversity. In this context, the reforms are regarded as part of a wider retreat from modern, bureaucratised state education systems. Such systems are perceived as having failed to fulfil their promise and now seem inappropriate to the heterogeneous societies of the 21st century. Thus moves towards diversity in schooling may reflect the needs of particular communities and interest groups brought into existence as a result of complex contemporary patterns of political, economic and cultural differentiation, which intersect the traditional class divisions upon which common systems of mass education were predicated.

In so far as these new divisions and emergent identities are experienced as real, they are likely to generate aspirations that will differ from traditional ones. Hence some of the attraction of current policies which I mentioned earlier. From the more optimistic readings of postmodernity, it is possible to contrast postmodernity with the oppressive uniformity of much modernist thinking as 'a form of liberation, in which the fragmentation and plurality of cultures and social groups allow a hundred flowers to bloom' (Thompson, 1992: 225–6). Some feminists, for example, have seen attractions in the shift towards the pluralist models of society and culture associated with postmodernism and postmodernity (Flax, 1987). The real possibilities for community-based welfare, rather than bureaucratically controlled welfare, are also viewed positively by some minority ethnic groups. At least until recently, Moslem groups in Britain had great hopes of the reforms. Thus, some aspects of the new policies did seem to connect to the aspirations of groups who had found little to identify with in the 'grand master' narratives associated with class-based politics. Support for schools run on a variety of principles might, then, be seen as recognising a widespread collapse of a commitment to modernity. Put another way, we said, the reforms might be viewed as a rejection of totalising narratives and their replacement by 'a set of cultural projects united [only] by a self proclaimed commitment to heterogeneity, fragmentation and difference' (Boyne and Rattansi, 1990: 9).

However, as we noted in Chapter 3, there is now considerable empirical evidence that, rather than benefiting the disadvantaged, the emphasis on parental choice and school autonomy in the British reforms has further disadvantaged those unable to compete in the market (Smith and Noble, 1995). At the same time, it is increasing the differences between popular and less popular schools on a linear scale – reinforcing a vertical hierarchy of schooling types rather than horizontal diversity (Whitty, 1994). There is therefore a real danger that the outcome will be a system which, far from being variously differentiated through the 'free' interplay of market forces, is increasingly stratified. In this situation, there is likely to be a disproportionate representation of socially advantaged children in the most 'successful' schools, and of socially disadvantaged children in those schools identified as 'failing'.

In our book (Whitty et al., 1993), we pointed out that in Britain such tendencies could have disastrous consequences for some sections of the predominantly working-class and black populations living in the inner cities. We conceded that these groups never gained an equitable share of educational resources under social-democratic policies, but the abandonment of planning in favour of a quasi-market could not be assumed to provide a fairer outcome. To regard the current espousal of heterogeneity, pluralism and local narratives as indicative of a new social order seemed to us to mistake phenomenal forms for structural relations. Marxist critics of theories of postmodernism and postmodernity, such as Callinicos (1989), who reassert the primacy of the class struggle, certainly take this view.

We concluded that, although current education policies may seem to be a response to changing economic, political and cultural priorities in modern societies, it would be difficult to argue, at least in the case of Britain, that they should be read as indicating that we have entered into a qualitatively new phase of social development – or experienced a postmodern break. Despite new forms of accumulation, together with some limited changes in patterns of social and cultural differentiation, the continuities seem just as striking as the discontinuities.

However, there is, as Michael Apple and I have argued (Apple and Whitty, 1999), a real danger that conceptual discontinuities within the sociology of education will make it more difficult to recognise this. With the growth of postmodern and poststructural literature in educational studies, we have perhaps tended to move rather too quickly away from earlier traditions of sociological analysis. Aspects of the new perspectives – rejection of the illusion that there can be one grand narrative under which all relations of domination can be subsumed, the focus on the 'pragmatic' and on the 'micro-level' as a site of the political, the illumination of the complexity of the power–knowledge nexus, the extension of our political concerns beyond the 'holy trinity' of class, gender, and race, the stress on multiplicity and heterogeneity, the idea of the decentred subject where identity is both non-fixed and a site of political struggle, and the focus on the politics and practices of consumption as well as production – have certainly been helpful. However, the fact that concepts such as social class do not explain all should not be used as an excuse to deny their power.

Although what we mean by class and how it is mobilised as a category need to be continually deconstructed and rethought, this does not mean that class is redundant as a sociological concept. And, ironically, it is one that may well help us to make sense of attempts by politicians, including John Major and Tony Blair, who seek, for their own electoral purposes, to deny or downplay its contemporary importance (Aronowitz, 1992). Thus, while I do not necessarily agree with Philip Wexler (1992) that class difference is always the overriding organising code of social life in schools and the larger society, its marginalisation in critical work in education may deny us one of the most potent analytic tools for making sense of current developments. Capitalism may be being transformed (though probably not entirely in the ways suggested by either politicians or various 'post-ist' theorists), but it remains a massive structuring force. Many people may not think and act in ways predicted by class-essentialising theories, but this does *not* mean that the structures of the racial, sexual, and class divisions of paid and unpaid labour have disappeared, nor does it mean that relations of production (both economic and cultural) can be ignored in understanding education (Apple, 1996).

The State and Civil Society

Similarly, as far as the policy response to social change is concerned, the dialectic of continuity and change is well-captured by the term 'conservative modernization', used by Roger Dale (1990) to characterise a policy which entails 'freeing individuals for economic purposes while controlling them for social purposes'. This was a key feature of the Thatcher government's education policy and, though perhaps with different social purposes, also that of New Labour. Rather than recent policies representing a 'postmodern break', neoconservative and neoliberal policies continue to vie with each other and with the residue of traditional social democratic approaches to educational reform.

Nevertheless, there clearly have been changes in the state's mode of regulation, even if we see current policies as new ways of dealing with old problems. Various new types of school in England – and equivalent quasi-autonomous institutions in other parts of the world – are now operating alongside, and increasingly in place of, collective provision by elected bodies with a mandate to cater for the needs of the whole population. Similar reforms have been introduced into the health and housing fields. With the progressive removal of tiers of democratically elected government or administration between the central state and individual institutions, conventional political and bureaucratic control by public bodies is replaced by quasi-autonomous institutions with devolved budgets competing for clients in the marketplace – a system of market accountability sometimes assisted by a series of directly appointed agencies, trusts and regulators. These administrative arrangements for managing education and other public services can be seen as new ways of resolving the problems of accumulation and legitimation facing the state in a situation where the traditional Keynesian 'welfare state' is no longer deemed to be able to function effectively (Dale, 1989).

Such quasi-autonomous institutions, state-funded but with considerable private and voluntary involvement in their operation, appear to make education less of a political issue. The political rhetoric accompanying the educational reforms in Britain certainly sought to suggest that education had been taken out of politics as normally understood. A former Conservative Education Minister, John Patten, argued that one of their aims was to 'depoliticise' education by removing it from the local political arena and giving power to parents and school governors (Riddell, 1992).

Manfred Weiss (1993) doubts that such reforms will be successful in deflecting responsibility for educational decision-making from the state to market forces and atomised individuals and units operating within civil society. In practice, anyway, recent education reforms in Britain are as much to do with transferring power from the local state to the central state as with giving autonomy to the schools. Nevertheless, governments can make cuts in education expenditure and blame the consequences on poor school management practices. This is a characteristic feature of how the new public administration actually works in practice, while appearing to devolve real power from the state to the market and agencies of civil society.

For this reason, I think I would now want to say that, although the extent of any underlying social changes can easily be exaggerated by various 'post-ist' forms of analysis, both the discourse and the contexts of political struggles in and around education have been significantly altered by the reforms. Not only have changes in the nature of the state influenced the reforms in education, the reforms in education are themselves beginning to change the way we think about the role of the state and what we expect of it. In his important historical study of *Education and State Formation* in England, France and the USA, my colleague Andy Green (1990) has pointed to the way in which education has not only been an important part of state activity in modern societies, but also played a significant role in the process of state formation itself in the eighteenth and nineteenth centuries. What I would now want to argue is that current changes in education policy are themselves linked to a redefinition of the nature of the state and a reworking of the relations between state and civil society.

The growing tendency to base more and more aspects of social affairs on the notion of consumer rights rather than upon citizen rights involves more than a move away from publicly provided systems of state education towards individual schools competing for clients in the marketplace. While seeming to respond to critiques of impersonal over-bureaucratic welfare state provision, this also shifts major aspects of education decision-making out of the public into the private realm with potentially significant consequences for social justice. Atomised decision-making within an already stratified society will actually reduce the possibility of collective struggles that might help those least able to help themselves. As Henry Giroux and Peter McLaren (1992) put it, 'competition, mobility, getting access to information, dealing with bureaucracies, providing adequate health and food for one's children are not simply resources every family possesses in equal amounts'. Because of this, the transfer of major aspects of educational decision-making from the public to the private realm undermines the scope for defending the interests of disadvantaged individuals and groups and thereby potentially intensifies those groups' disadvantage.

As the new education policies foster the idea that responsibility for welfare, beyond the minimum required for public safety, is to be defined entirely as a matter for individuals and families, then not only is the scope of the state narrowed, but civil society will be progressively defined solely in market terms. In fact, as Foucault reminds us in one of his interviews, one of the many origins of the concept of civil society was the attempt by late eighteenth-century liberal economists to protect an autonomous economic sphere in order to limit the growing administrative power of the state (Kritzman, 1988). Some of the radical educators of the 1960s and 1970s would have shared this wish for a set of social relations not prescribed by state regulation. But they would have had a different concept of civil society, regarding it more in terms of a public sphere in which common, as opposed to particular, interests are expressed in social movements, the realm if you like of active citizenship.

But as education appears to be devolved from the state to an increasingly marketised civil society, consumer rights will prevail over citizen rights. This will reduce the opportunities for democratic debate and collective action. Janet McKenzie (1995) argues that education has increasingly been excluded from the public sphere in Britain, though she also suggests that it has never been firmly established within a popular discursive arena. The contrast between the popular response to attacks on publicly provided education in Britain and France perhaps demonstrates that, in certain conditions, the tradition of citizen rights in education may be sufficiently strong to resist the trends in education policy we have experienced in Britain, the USA, New Zealand and parts of Australia. Similarly, Andy Green (1994) did not see what he called the 'neo-liberal' or 'post-modern turn' in education policy as having much appeal in countries with effective state educational systems, including Japan and much of continental Europe. Even though more recent developments in some of those countries may lead to some revision of that view at the margins, Green is surely right that such countries are unlikely to abandon the key role of planned education systems in fostering social solidarity and national cohesion.

However, social solidarity and national cohesion are not the same thing as democratic citizenship rights. In Britain, certain aspects of state intervention were maintained, indeed strengthened, by the Thatcher government's National Curriculum. As we saw in Chapter 2, England's National Curriculum specified programmes of study and attainment targets for the three 'core' subjects, English, mathematics and science, and seven other 'foundation' subjects. While some of the extreme neoliberals of the New Right would have liked to see the curriculum itself left to the market, the Thatcher government was rather more convinced by the argument of neo-conservative pressure groups, such as the Hillgate Group. This group argued that, even if market forces should ultimately be seen as the most desirable way of determining a school's curriculum, central government imposition of a National Curriculum on all state schools was a necessary interim strategy to undermine the vested interests of a 'liberal educational establishment' which threatened educational standards and traditional values.

So, while happy to see the emergence of new and autonomous schools, including Islamic schools and such other schools as parents desired, the Hillgate Group's – and the Thatcher government's – commitment to market forces was in the context of an insistence that all children 'be provided with the knowledge and understanding that are necessary for the full enjoyment and enhancement of British society'. 'Our' culture, being part of the universalistic culture of Europe, they suggested, 'must not be sacrificed for the sake of a misguided relativism, or out of a misplaced concern for those who might not yet be aware of its strengths and weaknesses' (Hillgate Group, 1987).

This assimilationist view sits uneasily with the expressed commitment to diversity and choice which attracted Moslem support for the Thatcher and Major governments, but has been a consistent feature of government policy symbolised in the notorious title of a 1980s report *West Indian Children in Our Schools* (my emphasis). Similar ideas clearly influenced the Thatcher government's insistence that the history programme of study within the National Curriculum should emphasise British and European history, as well as its undisguised dissatisfaction with the proposals initially brought forward by a working group on the programme of study for English which were seen as insufficiently concerned with English grammar and the established canon of English literature (Whitty, 1992a).

Thus, while supporting a degree of parental choice, neoconservatives were particularly concerned to support those 'who defend the traditional values of Western societies, and in particular who recognize that the very universalism and openness of European culture is our best justification for imparting it, even to those who come to it from other roots' (Hillgate Group, 1987). Such discourse thus worked both to acknowledge difference and to defuse its potential challenge to the prevailing social order. It clearly differentiates cultures on a hierarchical basis which sees social progress largely in terms of assimilation into European culture. Given its influence on British government policies at the time the Education Reform Act was being finalised, the reading of those policies as a reflection of the sort of postmodern society which celebrates heterogeneity and difference becomes even more questionable, though it might be argued that the National Curriculum has commodified 'tradition' and an 'imagined past'. Certainly, through its selection of content and modes of assessment, the original National Curriculum in England tended to promote an individualistic, hierarchical and nationalistic culture rather than an open and tolerant society.

In terms of educational decision-making, the example of the National Curriculum suggests that it is not merely that the contemporary state has devolved responsibility to a re-marketised civil society. In the British case, it may have abdicated some responsibility for ensuring social justice by deregulating major aspects of education, but in increasing a limited number of state powers it has actually strengthened its capacity to foster particular interests while appearing to stand outside the frame. Janet McKenzie (1995) argues that British governments have actually increased their claims to knowledge and authority over the education system while promoting a theoretical and superficial movement towards consumer sovereignty and Kevin Harris (1993) has argued that this is more generally the case. Some aspects of education have been 'privatised' in the sense of transferring them to the private sphere; others have become a matter of state mandate rather than democratic debate. These education policies in Britain can thus be seen as part of that broader project to create a free economy and a strong state (Gamble, 1988). In other words, as far as democratic citizenship is concerned, this may even be the worst of both worlds.

Foucault, of course, warns us against the Manichaeism of seeing the state as bad and civil society, the sphere of voluntary association, as good (Kritzman, 1988). But we also have to be careful not to reverse that evaluation now that civil society is being marketised. There is sometimes a tendency for those of us who have criticised the role of the state in education in the past to suddenly present the state as the solution to the inequities of the market. Furthermore, a Gramscian view of civil society would warn us against seeing even non-marketised versions of civil society as purely the repository of citizenship rights and an effective counterbalance to the state. However, if all social relations are now becoming accommodated in the notion of the strong state and the free economy, then neither the state nor civil society will be the context of active democratic citizenship through which social justice can be pursued.

Reasserting Citizen Rights

Despite my reservations about the National Curriculum in England, it remains for the time being the one symbol of a common educational system and an identifiable entitlement which people can struggle collectively to alter in a situation where most other decisions are becoming individualised in an increasingly atomised society. But a more thorough-going and sustainable reassertion of citizenship rights in education would seem to require the development of a new public sphere between the state and a marketised civil society, if you like, in which new forms of collective association can be developed and eventually new forms of democratic governance themselves. Certainly in England under the Conservatives, far too much was left to the market, to be determined by the self-interest of some consumers and the competitive advantages of some schools, as some parents and some schools sought each other out in a progressive segmentation of the market. Meanwhile those public institutions that might have acted on behalf of the broader interests of the community were progressively dismantled.

In response to these developments, Michael Adler (1993a, 1993b), after chronicling the inequitable results of similar choice policies in Scotland, suggested some revisions to Conservative policies which would take choice seriously but avoid the most unacceptable consequences of the existing legislation. His particular proposals included retaining local education authorities with a responsibility for formulating admissions policies for all local schools; encouraging schools to develop distinctive characteristics; requiring positive choices on behalf of all children and not only the children of 'active choosers'; involving teachers and older pupils in making decisions which were not necessarily to be tied to parental preferences; and giving priority in over-subscribed schools to the applicants who were most strongly supported. This would necessitate the existence of contexts for determining such rules and processes for adjudicating between different claims and priorities.

Similar safeguards were recommended in an important OECD study of choice policies in England, Australia, the Netherlands, New Zealand, Sweden and the United States. This concluded that where there was a dominant model of schooling, choice was as likely to reinforce hierarchies as to improve educational opportunities and the quality of schooling. It is also argued that demand pressures were rarely enough to produce real diversity of provision, so that positive supply side initiatives were necessary to create real choice. To avoid reinforcing tendencies towards academic and social selection, popular schools may need positive incentives to expand and disadvantaged groups need better information, better transport and perhaps privileged access to certain schools (OECD, 1994). Again, all such suggestions entail the revival or creation of institutional contexts within which such issues can be determined.

Raymond Plant quite rightly rejects the neo-liberal claim that a market cannot operate unjustly because its outcomes are both unintended and unforeseeable for individuals, if it is foreseeable (as it is in the case of education in England) that those already disadvantaged are likely to be further disadvantaged by market provision, 'then we can be held to bear collective responsibility for the outcomes...[especially] when the outcomes are capable of being altered' (Plant, 1990). However, given what has been dismantled by New Right governments, creating a new public sphere in which educational matters can even be debated – let alone determined – poses considerable challenges. Foucault pointed out that what he called new forms of association, such as trade unions and political parties, arose in the nineteenth century as a counterbalance to the prerogative of the state, and that they acted as the seedbed of new ideas (Kritzman, 1988). We need now to consider what might be the modern versions of these collectivist forms of association to counterbalance not only the prerogative of the state, but also the prerogative of the market.

But if new approaches are to be granted more legitimacy than previous ones, what new institutions might help to foster them? Clearly, such institutions could take various forms and they will certainly need to take different forms in different societies. They will no doubt be struggled over and some will be more open to hegemonic incorporation than others. Some may actually be created by the state, as the realisation dawns that a marketised civil society itself creates contradictions that need to be managed. Thus there may well be both bottom-up and top-down pressure to create new institutional forms within which struggles over the control of education will take place.

At various times Community Education Forums or similar bodies have been favoured by the Labour Parties in England and New Zealand, but we will need to give more careful consideration to the composition, nature and powers of such forums if they are to provide an appropriate way of reasserting democratic citizenship rights in education in the early twenty-first century. They will also need to respond to critiques of the gender bias of conventional forms of political association in most modern societies. So, if we wish to replace the role of unaccountable individuals, agencies and private consultants in educational decision-making with representatives of legitimate interests, what forms of representation should we be calling for? Paradoxically, current forms of democracy in England may be even less appropriate than those associated with directly elected School Boards in the nineteenth century, which used 'an advanced form of proportional representation [which] ensured that all the major political and religious groupings could be represented on the School Boards, so that positive policies at this level achieved a genuine consensus' (Simon, 1994: 12).

We now have to ask what are the appropriate constituencies through which to express community interests in the new millennium? What forms of democracy can express the complexity of contemporary communities? If, as Chantel Mouffe (1992) suggests, a radical pluralist conception of citizenship involves creating unity without denying specificity, how can this actually be expressed?

A straightforward return to the old order of things would be neither feasible nor sensible. Social-democratic approaches to education which continue to favour the idea of a common school are faced with the need to respond to increasing specialisation and social diversity. As Bob Connell (1993) has reminded us, 'justice cannot be achieved by distributing the same amount of a standard good to children of all social classes... That "good" means different things to ruling class and working class children, and will do different things for them (or to them).'

James Donald (1990) once called for approaches based on 'participation and distributive justice rather than simple egalitarianism and on cultural heterogeneity rather than a shared humanity'. However, David Hargreaves (1994) argues that, while we should be happy to encourage a system of independent, differentiated and specialised schools, we should also reassert a sense of common citizenship by insisting on core programmes of civic education in all schools. My own view is that Hargreaves pays insufficient attention not only to the effects of the neoliberal reforms in exacerbating existing inequalities between schools and in society at large but also underestimates the power of the hidden curriculum of the market to undermine any real sense of commonality, as will be discussed in the next chapter. The very exercise of individual choice and school self-management can so easily become self-legitimating for those with the resources to benefit from it and the mere teaching of civic responsibility is unlikely to provide an effective counterbalance.

Most crucially, in view of what I have been saying here, the changing nature of modern societies not only requires changes in the nature of schools in the twenty-first century but also changes in the manner in which decisions are made about schools. If we are to avoid the atomisation of educational decision-making, and associated tendencies towards the fragmentation and polarisation of schooling, we need to create new contexts for determining appropriate institutional and curricular arrangements on behalf of the whole society. This will require new forms of association in the public sphere within which citizen rights in education policy – and indeed other areas of public policy – can be reasserted against current trends towards both a restricted version of the state and a marketised civil society. If we want equity to remain on the educational agenda, we should certainly be looking to find new ways of making educational decision-making a part of democratic life and a legitimate public sphere, rather than colluding with the death of public education – or even merely critiquing its demise. These issues are explored further in the next chapter, while the particular policies of New Labour are examined in the final chapters of the book.

Further Reading

Apple, Michael (1996) *Cultural Politics and Education*. Buckingham: Open University Press.

Halsey, A. H., Lauder, Hugh, Brown, Phillip and Stuart Wells, Amy (eds) (1997) *Education: Culture, Economy, Society*. Oxford: Oxford University Press.

Hill, Dave, McLaren, Peter, Cole, Mike and Rikowski, Glenn (eds) (1999) *Postmodernism in Educational Theory*. London: Tufnell Press.

6

The Overt and Hidden Curricula
of Quasi-Markets
with Sally Power

In this chapter, we argue that education policy, rather like the school curriculum, transmits both overt and hidden messages. We suggest that the hidden messages of market reforms may be at least as significant as the overt ones in constructing educational cultures and identities for a changing world order. At the same time, some of the overt messages seek to defend an older order based on apparently stable national cultures. We argue that some of the conceptual resources derived from the so-called 'new sociology of education' could be updated and invoked to help make sense of the contradictions and opportunities generated by these tensions.

Speaking at the Institute of Economic Affairs in London in 1988, Bob Dunn, Under-Secretary of State at the Department of Education and Science (DES) in Margaret Thatcher's government, speculated whether 'a study in the life and teachings of Adam Smith should be compulsory in all schools' (quoted in *Education*, 8 July 1988). Whether or not the irony was intended, there is little doubt that, one way or another, the ideas of free market advocates have been highly influential in restructuring public education in England and elsewhere. We have not yet seen the life and teachings of Adam Smith written into the school timetable, but we should not assume that the lessons of neoliberalism are not being learnt. We therefore look in this chapter at both the hidden and overt curricula of recent reforms and explore the extent to which schools are teaching new subjects – or even 'new right' subjects.

The Marketisation of Education

As we have seen earlier in the book, public education systems are in the process of rapid and far-reaching reforms. In many countries, a range of policies has been introduced that attempt to reformulate the relationship between government, schools and parents through the application of market forces. Not only England, Australia, New Zealand and the USA, but countries with quite different histories, such as Chile, Sweden and South Africa, are seeing the introduction of similar policies. It has been argued that this trend is related to a broader economic, political and cultural process of globalisation and to 'post-Fordism' and 'postmodernity', as discussed in Chapter 5. Whatever the ultimate significance of these transformations, there is general agreement that the role of the nation state is in a process of change, although Dale (1994) rightly reminds us that a whole set of political-economic variables will affect the ways in which different education systems respond to processes of globalisation.

The implications of these changes for the provision of education are likely to be profound. Much research has focused on the impact which the dismantling of public education will have on efficiency, effectiveness and equity, but it is also likely to influence the nature of educational transmissions. The link between corporate involvement in schools, the structure and governance of schools and the form and content of the messages they transmit to their students will not be straightforward, but its significance should not be underestimated.

Green (1997) suggests that the marketisation of education and concomitant reduction in state intervention will lead to a lack of social cohesion which may weaken economic development. Others, however, suggest that education systems are teaching new forms of identity that are more appropriate to these new times. Nation states, they submit, no longer need disciplined workers and loyal recruits. Globalisation obviates the need for ideologies which unambiguously assimilate the local to the national. On this argument, the old order is swept away with the advent of the transnational economy.

A Corporate Curriculum?

One indicator of the alleged ascendancy of the global marketplace over tradition and culture might be the increasing presence of corporate interests in the classroom. It has been argued that the liberal humanism of the curriculum is gradually but inexorably being superseded by the neoliberal consumerism promulgated by business and industry. Whereas the school curriculum has traditionally transcended – indeed actively distanced itself from – the world of commerce, the marketisation of education is forging a new intimacy between these two domains.

Commercial penetration of the curriculum is evident in many countries. In America, for instance, the commercial satellite network Channel One offers schools free monitors on condition that 90 per cent of students watch its news and adverts almost every day. Molnar (1996) cites a wide range of examples where corporate business entices schools to promote their products. In the UK, as in the USA, there are schemes whereby equipment can be purchased with vouchers from supermarket chains, the take-up of which is enhanced as a result of budget constraints and the removal of public control (Roberts, 1994). In addition, there has been a proliferation of commercially sponsored curriculum materials to the extent that, in Britain, an independent organisation designed to protect consumer interests has seen fit to publish a good practice guide for teachers, governors, LEAs and parents (National Consumer Council, 1996).

Sometimes the objective of this commercial penetration seems to be product familiarisation, but curriculum materials can also be used to portray a partial, and inaccurate, account of business interests and impact. Molnar (1996) quotes a study guide on banking which defines 'free enterprise' as the symbol of 'a nation which is healthy and treats its citizens fairly'. Harty's international survey of corporate products in the classroom found that 'the biggest polluters of the environment – the chemical, steel, and paper industries – were the biggest producers of environmental education material' (1994: 97).

Critics fear that the commercialisation of education will not only lead children to adopt an uncritical approach to corporate activities, it will also damage the cultural work of the school. In common with many critiques of what is sometimes called 'McDonaldisation', commercialisation is seen to impoverish cultural heritage. Harty (1994) believes that schools will develop 'an anti-intellectual emphasis' and 'a consumptionist drive to purchase status goods'. Indeed, she alleges that the permeation of multinationals 'contributes to a standardised global culture of material gratification... [which will] impinge on the cultural integrity of whole nations' (Harty, 1994: 98–9). In this scenario, far from encouraging students to appreciate the particularities of their regional or national inheritance, schooling is about the training of desires, rendering subjects open to the seduction of ever-changing consumption patterns and the politics of lifestyling.

While the presence of corporate interests in the classroom needs to be treated as a cause for some concern, we should be careful not to overstate the extent to which they have squeezed out more conventional school activities. Corporate interests are penetrating the educational domain to a greater extent than hitherto – but there is no evidence of a business takeover. Many of the corporate-financed schools in the USA have now been incorporated into the public sector (Molnar, 1996). The Edison Project, mentioned above, reduced its plans for a nationwide chain of schools to four after it managed to raise only $12 million of the $2.5 billion originally envisaged. In Britain, the City Technology College initiative – held up as auguring a new partnership between business and education – was supposed to be funded primarily by private companies. In the event, the government found it extremely difficult to secure sponsorship, which at best amounted to 20 per cent of capital expenditure with public funds making up the shortfall (Whitty et al., 1993). There have subsequently been similar problems with Education Action Zones.

We should also be cautious about presuming that the messages of the multinationals are 'successfully' received. It is possible to imagine classes in which teachers make the relationship between business and education problematic. The ethics of encouraging children to shop at particular supermarkets has no doubt already been widely debated by students and teachers. It is hard to envisage health educators not pointing out the ironies of fast food manufacturers promoting good health guides. Similarly, curriculum materials designed by multinationals can be used to highlight omissions and distortions and expose the vested interests of their producers. This does not mean we should be complacent about the commercialisation of the curriculum – as Harty points out many teachers do not discuss the commercial origins and implications of the materials, an aspect which is likely to increase as teachers cope with all the other pressures of devolution and marketisation.

Nevertheless, the process of inculcating these new values and desires is unlikely to be straightforward. There is more evidence of increased involvement of business and industry within marketised education systems than in the earlier system based on public control, but the messages promoted by commercial sponsorship tend to be highly visible. This visibility makes them more accessible to interrogation and, therefore, potentially less insidious than other aspects of marketisation. It may be more subtle shifts in the form and governance of schooling as much as changes in the content of the overt curriculum which reposition subjects.

Learning from Marketised Relations

The marketisation of education has changed relations between and within schools in a number of ways which can be seen to reflect and reorient students tacitly within new phases of consumption and production. Ball claims that 'insofar as students are influenced and affected by their institutional environment then the system of morality "taught" by schools is increasingly well accommodated to the values complex of the enterprise culture' (1994: 146). Old values of community, cooperation, individual need and equal worth, which Ball claims underlay public systems of comprehensive education, are being replaced by marketplace values that celebrate individualism, competition, performativity and differentiation. These values and dispositions are not made visible and explicit, but emanate from the changing social context and permeate the education system in myriad ways. They can thus be seen to constitute the hidden curriculum of marketised relations.

One facet of the changed institutional environment is the fragmentation of national and state systems of common schooling in the desire to encourage diversity on the supply side. In Britain, as we saw in Chapter 3, the government has made a number of provisions for specialist schools. City Technology Colleges (CTCs) were intended to be new secondary schools for the inner city, with a curriculum emphasis on science and technology. Other schools have been encouraged, originally by the Conservatives but now by New Labour, to emphasise specialised curriculum provision, for instance in sports or languages.

In England, CTCs appear to be in the 'vanguard' of such a transformation with their 'shopping mall' or 'business park' architecture designed to emulate the world of finance (Whitty et al., 1993). Gewirtz et al. (1995) provide a semiological analysis of the impact of market reforms and comment on the 'glossification' of school imagery. Many of their case study schools had revamped reception areas to enhance the 'corporate' image of the school, installing fittings that would previously have been associated with banking and commerce. Principals were concerned to promote the 'corporate colours' of the school – even, as in one case, extending to the colour of the gas taps in the new science laboratories.

In the USA, applications for charter schools status have been made for schools such as the Global Renaissance Academy of Distinguished Education, EduPreneurship and the Global Academy for International Athletics (Molnar, 1996) – in addition to the many magnet school initiatives. Plans for the Edison Project schools incorporated a high tech image of the school of the future 'where each student will have a computerised learning station, without textbooks or classrooms, and each teacher will have an office, just like real people – with phones' (Tennessee Education Association News, cited in Molnar, 1996: 159). Some believe that the physical dimension of 'going to school' will eventually be lost altogether. Perhaps in correspondence with the rise of 'homeworking', Usher and Edwards (1994) speak of a 'reconfiguration' of the regulation of students who will no longer be required to attend educational institutions at all.

While it is hard to envisage the disestablishment of schooling in the near future, it is often considered that technological innovations are beginning to transform the social relations of education. Kenway et al. (1998) talk of a new pedagogy which can be characterised by 'infinite lateral connectedness' and 'vertical porousness'. Old hierarchies and boundaries will be swept aside as schools develop less directional modes of learning. Corresponding to alleged changes in the workplace (Mumby and Stohl, 1991), relationships between staff and between staff and students will move towards a 'flatter' structure. The boundary between home and school will also be eroded through the development of cross-site learning based on computer technologies. The high status conventionally accorded to print-based culture will be reduced as more high tech modes of knowledge production and transmission come 'on line'. In contrast to traditional conceptions of education which emphasise initiation into sacred bodies of knowledge, the nexus between teacher and pupil is restructured so that, in the words of Usher and Edwards, educative processes need only 'constitute a relationship between producer and consumer where knowledge – quantities of information – is exchanged on the basis of the value it has to the consumer, and in which consumers commodify their "experience" in exchange for qualifications' (Usher and Edwards, 1994: 174).

Despite the initial plausibility of these arguments, closer examination of empirical evidence does not justify claims of such sweeping transformations, certainly at the level of compulsory education. At the system level, diversity and specialisation within education provision remain objectives rather than reality. Attempts to diversify provision have been a good deal less innovative than promised and have tended to reinforce, rather than diminish, hierarchies between schools. Moreover, certainly within England, it is important to note that these 'new' kinds of school have been government, rather than market-led, initiatives. There is little indication that recent reforms have modified the distinctions which are commonly made between 'bad', 'good' and 'better' schools. And, as we have seen, far from introducing horizontal forms of differentiation, all the evidence thus far suggests that marketisation of education leads to an increase in vertical differentiation – exaggerating linear hierarchies through traditional rather than alternative criteria.

Changes in social relations *within* schools, as discussed in Chapter 4, are hardly unambiguously post-Fordist. Evidence of the arrival of a 'new' pedagogy is even harder to find. Although at one level schools are becoming more 'business-like' in approach and appearance, many are placing a renewed emphasis on pupil dress and authoritarian modes of discipline. Halpin et al. (1997) found a reinvigorated traditionalism in which relationships between staff and students were more, rather than less, formal and hierarchical. Some research also shows that reform has led to greater tracking within schools. Gewirtz et al. (1995) found increasing segregation of 'able' children and a move from mixed ability grouping towards setting in almost all their case study schools. It is true that new technologies are rapidly finding their way into schools, but there is little evidence that they are contributing to a shift from teaching to a culture which emphasises pupil-directed learning. Even in those centres of innovation – the CTCs – lessons tended to be conducted along conventional lines with few instances of new technologies being used outside IT lessons (Whitty et al., 1993) – an aspect also noted by Kenway et al. (1998) in their own research. Far from seeing new technologies as the start of a new and different epoch of learning, Apple (1986) has argued that we should recognise them as part of an intensifying process of proletarianisation and deskilling.

The connection between performance and accountability within marketised education systems has tended to lead to the fragmentation and delineation of curriculum content and a reduction in teacher and learner autonomy. In parallel with criticisms of other centralised curricula, Robertson and Soucek's research (reported in Robertson, 1993) within a Western Australian secondary school found that the new curriculum '...was at the same time both highly tailored and modularized into consumable packages and excessively assessed' (1993: 129). They claim '[t]hese features worked to compartmentalize school learning and teaching, as well as to develop an intense sense of alienation between the student and the teachers...exaggerating the reductive, technocratic and fragmented nature of much school knowledge' (1993: 129–30).

A New Correspondence?

It is striking how reminiscent these words are of the work of Bowles and Gintis (1976) on their so-called 'correspondence thesis'. Writing twenty years ago, they too pointed to a structural correspondence between the social relations of the educational system and those of production in which:

> ...relationships between administrators and teachers, teachers and students, students and students, and students and their work – replicate the hierarchical division of labour. Hierarchical relations are reflected in the vertical authority lines from administrators to teachers to students. Alienated labour is reflected in the student's lack of control over his or her education, the alienation of the student from curriculum content, and the motivation of school work through a system of grades and other external rewards... Fragmentation in work is reflected in the institutionalized and often destructive competition among students through continual and ostensible meritocratic ranking and evaluation.
>
> (Bowles and Gintis, 1976: 131)

The apparent similarity between Bowles and Gintis' analysis and more recent accounts, such as those of Robertson and Soucek, begs a number of questions. First, it raises the issue of whether schools are still engaged in the production of 'old' rather than 'new' subjectivities. More specifically, are marketised education systems simply a new way of producing 'old' subjects? Such a position would presumably be supported by those who argue that the marketisation of public education is a state-initiated response to the recurrent problem of legitimating the mode of production, and the state's role within it, at a time of crisis in capital accumulation (see Dale, 1989; Weiss, 1993).

If so, this would suggest that the case for claiming 'new times' is less than convincing. Hirst and Thompson (1996) certainly claim that there is nothing particularly new about the current degree or rate of international interaction which has always been, and still is, patchy and sporadic rather than the more universal and inexorable process implied by globalisation theorists. Even if we concede that there has been a reduction in the profile of the nation state as an international entity, there is nothing to suggest that it is weakening its grip on areas of internal regulation.

However, even if recent changes are less ground-breaking than some social theorists suggest, this does not mean that the picture is only one of continuity. Marketised education systems provide evidence of both changes and continuities which appear to both match and contradict other social trends. This lack of correspondence between education systems and the wider social and economic context may result from delayed response or complete structural disarticulation. Delayed response arguments are perhaps more convincing than those that go for complete disarticulation. At the level of further and higher education, in particular, it is possible to see a commodification of learning packages, a drive towards 'pick and mix' courses which have been described as a 'cafeteria curriculum' and a degree of de-institutionalisation with the growth of distance learning through new technologies. It could be argued that these changes are only evident at the margins rather than in the core of the education system, and that the central structure and function of the compulsory phases remain unchanged.

On the other hand, any claims for the distinctiveness of the compulsory dimension of public education may be increasingly difficult to sustain. There has been some debate among neoliberals on the merits of disestablishing schools (Tooley, 1995). But even if schools retain their institutional location, it is perhaps only a matter of time before they experience the changes which are taking place in the later phases. Nor would acknowledging such correspondence necessarily mean making a wholesale commitment to the kind of correspondence principle expounded by Bowles and Gintis. As Bailey comments, 'it may be that correspondence does not have universal applicability, but nevertheless is an insightful idea to apply to certain places and at certain times' (1995: 482). Indeed, Hickox and Moore (1992) argue that stronger claims can be made for correspondence under post-Fordism than the system of mass production analysed by Bowles and Gintis.

Nevertheless, we should be cautious in presuming that schools will successfully mould the future citizens and consumers required for the 'new times'. The publicly controlled national education systems may have produced disciplined workers and local recruits, but they also produced other sorts of dispositions that appear less than functional to the needs of capital. As Bernstein pointed out in 1977: 'Consider various forms of industrial action over the last hundred years. The school in this respect is highly inefficient in creating a docile, deferential and subservient workforce. The school today has difficulty in disciplining its pupils' (Bernstein, 1977: 187–8).

It might be argued that if education systems had problems fulfilling the relatively simple tasks of Fordist modes of production, how much more difficult to create the kind of flexible postmodern subjects apparently required within the global marketplace. However, it could be claimed that the erosion of the collectivities characteristic of systems of mass production will facilitate the interpellation of subjects within the new order. If opposition arises out of collective action and awareness, as has traditionally been held by theorists on the left, then the atomised and flexible consumers of marketised education may be unable to counteract the penetrating individualisation of global markets. On the other hand, we should be careful not to misrepresent the nature and impact of earlier modes of collective engagement. Past solidarities were often more imagined than real. As Featherstone (1995) demonstrates, accounts of working-class life, both in sociology and popular culture, typically overplay its homogeneity and capacity for communal bonding. They also frequently overlook the sexual and racial basis of exclusion and inclusion within such 'solidarities'. Theoretically, conceptions of the decentred subject and radical pluralism also undermine the notion of 'fixed' identities and enduring allegiances.

The Role of the State

Nevertheless, as England's National Curriculum demonstrates, attempts to foster identification with specific 'real' or 'imagined' communities remain an important element of contemporary education policy. Even though the 'old order' of national, class and gender identities may be being fractured in some respects through the ravages of neoliberalism, neoconservative policies are meanwhile encouraging schools to engage more explicitly than ever before in the promotion of tradition and nationhood. Despite attempts by governments to attract support for schools from business and industry, there is little to suggest that the state is prepared to relinquish control of the curriculum. Usher and Edwards' confident claim that in these new times 'the state plays less and less of a role' (1994: 175) is just not borne out by evidence. Although some other countries have perhaps not been as prescriptive as Britain, many governments at state or national level have tightened their control over the curriculum in terms of what is taught and/or how this is to be assessed.

Central regulation of the curriculum is not only geared towards standardising performance criteria in order to facilitate professional accountability and consumer choice within the education marketplace, it is also about creating, or recreating, forms of national identity. As we saw earlier, the formulation of the National Curriculum in England has been underlain by a consistent requirement that schools concentrate on British history, British geography and 'classic' English literature. Far from reflecting a loosening of geographic boundaries, a diminution of the specificity of the nation state or the increasing interpenetration of cultures characteristic of globalisation, such curriculum reforms represent a conscious attempt to position subjects in ways which hark backwards to some imagined past, rather than forwards into new globalised times. As Stuart Hall comments '... at the very moment when the so-called material basis of the old English identity is disappearing over the horizon of the West and the East, Thatcherism brings Englishness into a more firm definition, a narrower but firmer definition than it ever had before.' (Hall, 1991: 25). The global marketplace may be, as Marquand (1995) claims, 'contemptuous of tradition, hostile to established hierarchies and relativist in morality' – but the visions of little England (or smalltown America) conjured up by New Right curricula certainly are not.

Thus, it is clear that any anti-traditional and relativist messages emanating from the market context need to be offset against those which are underscored by New Right governments highlighting the inalienable rights to national sovereignty, the inviolability of 'our' cultural heritage and the absolutism of traditional (often nineteenth century) morality. This tension is evident, but also accommodated, within the contrasting messages of the overt and the hidden curriculum. While at the level of direct transmissions students are to be taught the values of the cultural restorationists (Ball, 1990), the context in which they are taught may undermine their canons. While the content of the lessons emphasises heritage and tradition, the form of their transmission is becoming increasingly commodified within the new education marketplace.

The need to address the tension between the overt and hidden curriculum is apparent in discussions about alternatives to recent education reforms. As we saw earlier, concern that the 'subversive' tendencies of the global marketplace will erode national and communal values has led some to suggest that citizenship or personal and social education (PSE) should receive more attention in the formal curriculum. Andy Green's (1997) comparative research also leads him to suggest that schools will need to regenerate social cohesion 'as the social atomization induced by global market penetration becomes increasingly dysfunctional'. He argues that the current abdication on the part of governments from pursuing goals of social cohesion will need to be reversed: 'With the decline of socially integrating institutions and the consequent atrophy of collective social ties, education may soon again be called upon to stitch together the fraying social fabric'. This heralds a return to some of the issues discussed in Chapter 2 and it is clearly part of the agenda of the New Labour government in Britain.

If such initiatives are to be progressive in their effects, they will need to go further than David Hargreaves' (1994) proposal for civic education, mentioned in Chapter 5, since it is unlikely that merely adding a component to the timetable will provide an effective counterbalance to the permeating values of the marketplace. If much of the potency of the hidden curriculum derives from its invisibility, it would seem unlikely that its effects could be overcome by overt citizenship education alone. Countering the power of the hidden curriculum seems likely to require the development of new sets of relations both within schools and beyond them, so that students can experience responses to globalisation other than the currently dominant neoliberal and neoconservative ones. More specifically, if we want students to learn democratic citizenship we need to put in place structures that embody those principles (Apple and Beane, 1996). Active and inclusive conceptions of citizenship are unlikely to be successfully learned through just another subject in an already over-crowded curriculum. Only if they become a central aspect of the everyday experience of schools as learning communities is citizenship education likely to make a significant contribution to the development of deep democracy. There is at least some recognition of this in the approach to citizenship education currently being advocated by some of those involved in taking forward New Labour's decision to add citizenship to the National Curriculum (Alexander, 2001). How effective their efforts prove to be, especially in relation to the countervailing forces discussed in Chapter 2, remains to be seen.

Conclusion

Future developments aside, it is clear that debates on the impact of recent reforms on pupils are, at this stage, highly speculative. The main arguments which have been set out in this chapter concern the nature of educational transmissions, rather than the extent to which they are absorbed, appropriated or resisted. Featherstone's criticisms of theories of mass culture are also applicable to education systems in that they share 'a strong view of the manipulability of mass audiences by a monolithic system and an assumption of the negative cultural effects of the media as self evident, with little empirical evidence about how goods and information are used in everyday practices' (Featherstone, 1995: 115). Even if it were possible to identify the needs of the new global marketplace, these would be mediated at the level of the school, which has its own grammar of accommodation and resistance.

What is clear from this discussion is that the policies and practices of schools within marketised systems display many contradictory elements and paradoxical tendencies. Bernstein (1990) claims that the market-oriented pedagogy is a 'much more complex construction' than what he terms the 'autonomous visible pedagogy'. It is, he argues, 'a new pedagogic Janus' which 'recontextualises and thus repositions within its own ideology features of apparently oppositional discourses'. There have, of course, always been contradictory elements within schooling – at system and classroom level (Dale, 1989) – but few have seemed as acute as those we are witnessing at the present time.

In this situation, we need to explore the relative impact of globalisation and the imperatives of the nation state and the relationship between the hidden curriculum of the marketplace and the overt lessons on the timetable. In addressing these questions it might be important to return to some of the understandings which were developed in the aftermath of the so-called 'new directions' for the sociology of education (Young, 1971).

The work of Bernstein (1997) suggests ways in which such a task might be approached. He argues that the tensions that arise from the increasing deregulation of the economic field and the increasing regulation of what he terms the symbolic field are generating new forms of pedagogic identity. Education reforms are leading to the recontextualisation of elements of the 'retrospective' identity of old conservatism and the 'therapeutic identity' associated with the child-centred progressivism of the 1960s and 1970s to produce two new hybrids, the 'decentred market' identity and the 'prospective' identity.

The 'decentred market' identity embodies the principles of neoliberal-ism. It has no intrinsic properties, its form is dependent only upon the exchange value determined by the market. It is therefore contingent upon local conditions and is highly unstable. The 'prospective' pedagogic identity, on the other hand, attempts to 'recentre' through selectively incorporating elements of old conservatism. It engages with contemporary change, but draws on the stabilising tradition of the past as a counter-balance to the instability of the market. These two new pedagogic identities are therefore both complementary and contradictory. To some extent they can be seen to embody the tensions within the reforms discussed in this book. As the decentred market pedagogy seeks to foster 'new' subjects, the 'prospective' pedagogy seeks to reconstruct 'old' subjects, albeit selectively in response to the pressures of a new economic and social climate.

The extent to which such pedagogic identities are actually being fostered by the new reforms requires further theoretical and empirical explorations. Such explorations require us to look at both form and content, the message and the medium, the juxtaposition of different types of knowledge and the complex and differential ways in which school knowledge relates to the everyday worlds of school students. The complexity and contradictions of recent developments may make such a task even more difficult than it appeared in the 1970s, but it needs to be addressed if we are to understand the ways in which subjects are being positioned by current policies and develop effective alternative strategies for fostering 'progressive' rather than 'conservative' prospective identities.

Further Reading

Apple, Michael (2001). *Educating the Right Way. Markets, Standards, God and Equality*. New York: RoutledgeFalmer.

Green, Andy (1997). *Education, Globalisation and the Nation State*. London: Macmillan.

Molnar, Alex (1996). *Giving Kids the Business: the Commercialization of America's Schools*. Boulder, CO: Westview Press.

7

School Improvement and Social Inclusion: Limits and Possibilities[1]

This chapter begins with a recognition that, while the strong correlation between school failure and social disadvantage does not determine educational outcomes for particular individuals, its significance for education policy can hardly be overstated. It explores various attempts to counter social disadvantage through education and argues that education policy alone is unlikely to achieve the outcomes sometimes expected of it. The chapter then provides an assessment of how far New Labour's attempts at tackling social exclusion through 'joined up government' in England have gone towards developing policies that are likely to be effective in bucking the prevailing trends of the past century.

There is long-standing – and continuing – evidence that, overall, pupils from disadvantaged social backgrounds fare relatively badly within formal educational systems. It is also the case that Britain is one of the advanced industrial societies in which this tendency is most marked. While some outstanding individuals have achieved the highest levels despite (or, in some cases, motivated by) their inauspicious backgrounds, the overall social distribution of educational success and failure has remained depressingly consistent. There is a strong negative correlation between most measures of social disadvantage and school achievement, as even a cursory glance at the league tables of school results demonstrates.

Some commentators have taken the fact that some schools perform better than others in the same area to mean that schools have their salvation in their own hands regardless of the material and spiritual poverty of their surroundings. Indeed, such was the strength of this view that, in 1995, Smith and Noble argued that any suggestion that poverty caused educational failure had become 'almost a taboo subject in public policy debate' (1995: 133). Those who dared to mention the subject were branded defeatist or patronising for even considering that social background can make a difference. Since then, we have had a New Labour government, but something of the same attitude has remained.

The New Labour argument has been that poverty is not an excuse for failure and that schools should not use it as such. However, some aspects of policy, such as Education Action Zones, do recognise that multiple social disadvantage can be a reason for failure, if not an excuse, and that a greater degree of positive discrimination than has been fashionable in recent years may once again be justified. While welcoming this development, I want to enter a few caveats, along the lines suggested by the title of a recent New Zealand study on this topic: *Schools Making a Difference: Let's be Realistic!* (Thrupp, 1999). So I want to explore both the possibilities and the limitations of attempts to foster social inclusion by countering the impact of social disadvantage on educational achievement and/or using educational achievement to counter social disadvantage. I shall pay particular attention to the efficacy of the sorts of school improvement strategies that have been fashionable in recent years. In doing so, I shall be drawing upon an attempt by Peter Mortimore and myself to stand back and reflect upon just what can and cannot be gained by school-based improvement strategies (Mortimore and Whitty, 1997). In that paper, we argued that it should not just be assumed that such strategies will contribute to greater social inclusiveness and pointed to some of the conditions that need to be met if school improvement is not to perpetuate – or even exacerbate – the problem of disadvantage and social exclusion.

Remedies Tried

There have been a number of distinct educational approaches to breaking the cycle of disadvantage. One approach rests on the concept of meritocracy, which was the basis of the scholarship ladder introduced at the beginning of the last century, subsequent 11-plus selection procedures and, most recently, the assisted places scheme. It has also informed the thinking behind public examinations generally. The evidence from studies of social mobility shows that such a meritocratic approach does help overcome the effects of disadvantage by promoting some individuals with outstanding talents. What such studies also show, however, is that, although this works for some, it fails to do so for many more (Brown et al., 1997) and does nothing to improve the standard of education for those left behind.

The second approach has involved the use of compensatory mechanisms. These include individual benefits, such as free school meals, uniform grants and other special measures for low-income families. Compensatory mechanisms have also included the allocation of additional resources to schools, such as in the Educational Priority Area programmes of the 1960s and 1970s, when extra payments were made to schools with high proportions of disadvantaged pupils (Halsey, 1972; Smith, 1987). One drawback of such schemes is that some advantaged pupils gain access to extra resources within the chosen schools, while many disadvantaged pupils in other schools do not (Plewis, 1997). The local management formulae for schools approved by governments in recent years have anyway allowed relatively little scope for significant levels of positive discrimination.

The third approach involves the creation of specific intervention projects, which can be used with the disadvantaged with a view to accelerating their educational development. Examples of such projects include the High/Scope pre-school programme in the USA and the Reading Recovery Programme in New Zealand and then in the UK. Despite the enthusiastic support of teachers and local authorities in the UK for such projects, official support and hence widespread implementation was, under the Conservative government, extremely limited.

This meant the focus increasingly fell upon school improvement projects, including some supported by the Institute of Education. The central tenet of school improvement is that the responsibility for change must lie in the hands of the school itself (Stoll and Fink, 1996). In contrast to centrally driven projects, and the thinking behind some more recent policies, those working in school improvement believe that the head-teacher, staff and school governing body – having listened to any external advice – are best placed to decide how to improve their own institutions (Mortimore, 1996). A senior DfEE official once told me that they were delighted that educationists were pushing this approach in the 1980s, because it inadvertently bolstered the government's belief in school autonomy, choice and saving money.

Even so, school improvement policies were effective in some cases. The National Commission on Education (NCE, 1996) undertook a project designed to uncover how some schools with disadvantaged pupils had improved and succeeded against the odds. Maden and Hillman's (1996) discussion of the findings from all the case studies in the project emphasises the importance of: a leadership stance which builds on and develops a team approach; a vision of success which includes a view of how the school can improve; the careful use of targets; the improvement of the physical environment; common expectations about pupils' behaviour and success; and an investment in good relations with parents and the community. The project demonstrated that committed and talented heads and teachers can improve schools even if they contain a proportion of disadvantaged pupils. In order to achieve improvement, however, such schools have to exceed what could be termed 'normal' efforts. Members of staff have to be more committed and work harder than their peers elsewhere. What is more, they have to maintain the effort so as to sustain the improvement. There can be no switching on the 'automatic pilot' if schools are aiming to buck the trend. Some of the examples in the follow-up study (Maden, 2001) demonstrate just how fragile success can be in such circumstances.

We must therefore beware of the dangers of basing a national strategy for change on the efforts of outstanding individuals working in exceptional circumstances. It is worth noting, anyway, that attributing causal effects to particular initiatives in complex organisations such as schools is always likely to be difficult. It is also difficult to ensure that one is always 'comparing like with like', because there is not yet a suitable national database which brings together accurate intake and examination outcome data. It is to be hoped that we will eventually have some robust 'value added' data to enable us to determine whether and how some schools promote, to a much greater extent than others, the progress of the disadvantaged.

But the problems facing us are not just technical ones of measurement. Work in other traditions suggests that we should not expect miracles, at least on a large scale. As I mentioned in Chapter 1, my fellow sociologists of education have often been rather critical of work on school effectiveness and school improvement studies. Angus argues that their narrow focus 'shifts attention away from the nature of knowledge, the culture of schooling and, most importantly, the question of for whom and in whose interests schools are to be effective' (1993: 342). In similar vein, Hatcher (1996) demonstrates that work in this tradition has consistently played down the significance of social class, while Gillborn and Youdell (2000) show that some of the everyday practices derived from it have differential and inequitable effects for different minority ethnic groups.

Even if, in response, schools adopt the sorts of strategies advocated by the new sociology of education to challenge culturally loaded curricular knowledge and teaching methods and seek to eliminate assessment bias – and they certainly need to do that where appropriate – schools will continue to be affected by their role within a wider society that still maintains a powerful sense of social and cultural hierarchy. Important as they are, such changes at school level are unlikely to answer the criticism of school improvement work that it has tended to exaggerate the extent to which individual schools can challenge such structural inequalities.

While some schools can succeed against the odds, the possibility of them all doing so, year in and year out, still appears remote given that the long-term patterning of educational inequality has been strikingly consistent throughout the history of public education. Although there are different theories about how the social and cultural patterning of educational outcomes occurs (Goldthorpe, 1996), these patterns reflect quite closely the relative chances of different groups entering different segments of the labour market. Accordingly, while it might be possible, for example, for the ethos of a particular school to help transform the aspirations of a particular group of pupils within it, it seems highly unlikely that all schools could do this in the absence of more substantial social changes.

Probably the most depressing finding of all the research is that the relative performance of the disadvantaged has too often remained similar even when the absolute performance of such groups has improved. At primary level, Mortimore's *School Matters* (Mortimore et al., 1988a) found that no school reversed the usual 'within school' pattern of advantaged pupils performing better than the disadvantaged. However, some of the disadvantaged pupils in the most effective schools made more progress than their advantaged peers in the least effective schools and even did better in absolute terms. Yet, encouraging as this is, it would appear that, if all primary schools were to improve so that they performed at the level of the most effective, the difference between the overall achievement of the most advantaged social groups and that of the disadvantaged might actually increase.

Similarly, at secondary level, schools rarely overcome the relative differences between the performance of different social groups. Despite the optimism of some school improvement literature, it is still difficult to counter the conclusion to be drawn from *Fifteen Thousand Hours* (Rutter et al., 1979) that, if all schools improved to the level of the best schools on current criteria, the stratification of achievement by social class might well appear even starker than it is now. This would happen because socially advantaged children in highly effective schools would achieve even more than they might do in a less conducive environment and the gap between them and their less advantaged peers would increase. In those circumstances, theories of 'relative deprivation' would suggest that the social exclusion of disadvantaged groups, as well as a disproportionate incidence of disaffection among individuals from those groups, would continue despite any overall improvement.

The initial report of Michael Barber's Literacy Task Force (Literacy Task Force, 1997) contained figures that point to the existence of this problem but then effectively ignored it. Instead, the report stated that 'whether children learn to read well is a lottery in both advantaged and disadvantaged areas'. But, as Ian Plewis and Harvey Goldstein (1998: 18) have pointed out, this is misleading: 'Chance plays only one part in whether and when a child learns to read; there are also systematic effects of social class, income, gender and ethnicity on children's attainments.' David Reynolds, head of the government's Numeracy Taskforce, has recognised that so far school improvement has done little to address such inequalities, but argues for the 'creation of a technology of educational policy and practice that is so strong, so relentless, and so powerful that it outweighs the effects of outside school influences and helps bring all schools to high standards of achievement, independently of their different backgrounds and starting points' (Reynolds, 1997: 23). This is quite a claim!

To be fair, Reynolds (1997) recognises the need for a degree of positive discrimination, as does the government's revised Literacy Strategy. Yet the assumption still seems to be that school-centred measures themselves can overcome inequalities. But, while it may be important for schools to set themselves challenging goals for all their pupils, it is also important to be clear about the limits of purely school-based actions. 'Education, education, education' cannot be the only priorities and, even if they are, they cannot be achieved through education policy alone.

This issue is particularly important in the light of considerable evidence from a number of countries that the recent marketisation of education has sometimes enabled advantaged parents and advantaged schools to further enhance their relative advantage, thereby increasing educational inequalities and social polarisation (Whitty, Power and Halpin, 1998). Although, as mentioned in Chapter 3, some researchers have now suggested that the overall trend towards increased social polarisation may have been merely an initial effect of choice policies (Gorard and Fitz, 1998a), the jury remains out on the methodology used in this work (Noden, 2000). In addition, there seems little doubt that polarisation has taken place in many local education markets (Gibson and Asthana, 1998).

Furthermore, despite some outstanding exceptions, it remains the case that schools located in contexts of multiple disadvantage have overall levels of performance substantially below the national average and have hitherto tended to be relatively ineffective at boosting pupils' progress (Gray, 1998; Gibson and Asthana, 1998). The problems and dilemmas facing schools with large numbers of disadvantaged pupils, compared with those with advantaged intakes, are much greater than recent education policies have recognised (Proudford and Baker, 1995; Thrupp, 1995; Thrupp, 1999). As Gray (2001: 33) concedes, 'we don't really know *how much* more difficult it is for schools serving disadvantaged communities to improve because much of the improvement research has ignored this dimension – that it is more difficult, however, seems unquestionable.'

It therefore seems that, if social inclusion is to be a major policy aim, then alongside a commitment to raise standards for all, there need to be very strong measures to ensure that the rate of improvement at the bottom is greater than that at the top. Programmes and interventions that shift opportunities towards disadvantaged individuals, families and communities seem more likely to reduce educational and other inequalities than more broadly based initiatives catering for all. If we seek to reduce inequalities, rather than merely to raise standards overall, policies will need to be more effectively targeted towards disadvantaged groups than has previously been the case. And, unless there is a substantial increase in overall education spending, this will require a real transfer of resources from advantaged to disadvantaged groups.

Social Disadvantage

So why is social disadvantage so powerful in relation to education? 'The concept of social disadvantage is [itself] not easy to define partly because it is a relative concept, tied to the social context of time and place' (Mortimore and Blackstone, 1982: 3). Townsend (1996) sees poverty in the same relative way as '...the absence or inadequacy of those diets, amenities, standards, services and activities which are common or customary in society'. In these terms, despite the general improvement over recent years in most people's living standards, conditions have worsened for a significant minority. The number of people living in poverty (50 per cent of average national earnings or less) has shown a threefold increase since 1979 and now stands at one-quarter of the population (Walker and Walker, 1997). In Britain, the increasing difference between the 'haves' and the 'have nots' during the 1980s seems to have resulted partly from the effects of official policies. 'Britain stands out internationally in having experienced the largest percentage increase in income inequality between 1967 and 1992' (Dennehy et al., 1997: 280). The proportion of children living in poor households rose to 32 per cent compared to the European Union average of 20 per cent (Eurostat, 1997).

Social disadvantage impacts on education both directly and indirectly. It is frequently associated with poorer health. Children tend to be physically weaker and have less energy for learning than their peers. They are also more likely to be emotionally upset by the tensions in their lives. They are less likely to have the opportunity for study and for educational help at home. These are just the conditions in which children will be vulnerable to low levels of self-efficacy: 'an inability to exert influence over things that adversely affect one's life, which breeds apprehension, apathy, or despair' (Bandura, 1995: 1). They, in turn, will work against children's development as effective school learners and, ultimately, according to Wilkinson (1997), their chance of a long healthy life. Healthy societies appear to be not those with the highest absolute standards of living, but those with the smallest income differentials (Wilkinson, 1996).

I explored some of these connections for Sir Donald Acheson's Independent Inquiry into Inequalities in Health (Whitty, Aggleton, Gamarnikow and Tyrer, 1998). Data from the 1970 birth cohort study shows that those without educational qualifications are, at age 26, four times more likely to report poor general health (23 per cent) than those with the highest educational qualifications (6 per cent). There is also an inverse relationship between educational qualifications and depression, with very high levels of depression evident particularly among women without educational qualifications (Montgomery and Schoon, 1997). Another conclusion to be drawn from cohort studies is that 'children who do well in education tend strongly to make healthier choices in adult life in health related habits of diet, alcohol consumption, smoking and exercise' (Wadsworth, 1997a: 200). Hence there is something of a vicious circle.

Because so few studies have controlled adequately for relevant variables, the exact nature of the relationship between educational, health and other forms of disadvantage remains unclear. Nevertheless, many studies have drawn attention to the cumulative and multiplicative effects of low social class of origin, poor educational achievement, reduced employment prospects, low levels of psychosocial well-being and poor physical and mental health (Benzeval et al., 1995; Wilkinson, 1994, 1996). A recent BMA study showing a growing health gap between the children of advantaged and disadvantaged families therefore bodes ill for the future (BMA, 1999).

As might be expected, housing is also intimately connected with both health and education. A range of studies has shown that poor housing in general, and living in temporary accommodation in particular, has adverse consequences for the physical and psycho-social development of children. In terms of physical well-being, the Black Report established a causal relationship between type of housing tenure and health. Seven years later, the National Children's Bureau (1987) provided further evidence that poor housing and homelessness were detrimental to child health. Other research and surveys reveal that living in temporary accommodation, particularly bed and breakfast hotels, has negative health aspects (e.g. Howarth, 1987), which are likely to be anything but temporary (Morton, 1988). In addition to ill health (e.g. Furley, 1989; Woodroffe et al., 1993), poor housing adversely affects other aspects of a child's development, through limitations on play (Edwards, 1992) and lack of supportive social networks (Crane, 1990).

Small wonder, then, that research has clearly linked homelessness to lower pupil achievement. For example, Bassuk and Rosenburg (1988) found that 40 per cent of pupils from a sample of homeless families in the USA were failing or producing 'below average' work, and one-quarter were in 'special' classes. Kozol (1988) and Stronge (1992) found that children living in welfare hotels were from one to three grades behind their peers. British work has shown similar connections between poor housing and lack of educational progress. An early report from the National Child Development Study (1972) found that overcrowded housing and lack of basic amenities were clearly correlated with lower reading ages and arithmetical achievement at primary school. More recently, Stepien et al. (1996) found that the vocabulary development of homeless children was behind that of others. Some of our own research, funded by Shelter (Power, Whitty and Youdell, 1995), has tried to explore some of the processes that lie behind such patterns of disadvantage. Sadly, it showed that the nature and organisation of current services, and professional responses to disadvantaged groups, were often as much part of the problem as part of the solution.

For example, our own attempts to get information from education, housing and social services departments generated many instances of non-response, confusion and lack of consistency. In one case, our questionnaire was copied to two different departments of the same local authority, who sent back contradictory answers to the same questions. This is indicative of the kind of demarcated and fragmented bureaucracies which homeless families themselves have to confront when trying to obtain appropriate services. This not only presents them with practical difficulties, it also prevents policy-makers and service providers from seeing the multiple effects of their policies on 'whole' persons and households. There is little doubt that this makes it easier to 'pass off' responsibility to other sectors and influences the kind of provision homeless families receive. It also means that professional responses often have to take the form of crisis management rather than developing ongoing liaison and support.

Schools, as well as families, experience a range of problems when they have high numbers of pupils living in temporary accommodation. Nearly two-thirds of head teachers whose schools had homeless children attending reported that the high turnover of homeless pupils had a noticeable impact on pupil population. While the level of pupil turnover varies from school to school, many schools reported having registered far more individual children each year than indicated by the total school roll. Within schools with significant numbers of homeless children, notably those in close proximity to bed and breakfast hotels, hostels and homeless units, there were very high rates of pupil turnover with pupils arriving and leaving on an almost constant basis. Overall, governmental, institutional and interpersonal level processes and practices, underpinned by implicit and explicit assumptions and expectations of homeless families, act to compound significantly barriers to educational inclusion which homeless children face. Only when the issues are seen as interrelated and coordinated strategies developed is there any real likelihood of changing that situation.

Breaking the Cycle

Gerald Grace, Director of the Institute's Centre for Research and Development in Catholic Education, has argued that over the years too many urban education reformers (including school improvers) have been guilty of 'producing naive school-centred solutions with no sense of the structural, the political and the historical as constraints' (Grace, 1984: xii).

Peter Robinson has claimed that educational measures alone are unlikely to alleviate the impact of disadvantage and has criticised government targets on the grounds that 'a serious programme to alleviate child poverty might do far more for boosting attainment and literacy than any modest intervention in schooling' (Robinson, 1997: 17). Indeed, it might be argued that the best way of improving schools in disadvantaged areas would probably be to transpose some of the socio-economic features of the sorts of areas in which the majority of high performing schools are placed.

Unfortunately, education policies under Conservative governments underplayed this issue, even though A. H. Halsey pointed out over twenty years ago, on the basis of his studies of Education Priority Areas, that '...the teacher cannot reconstruct the community unaided...the needs of the neighbourhood for health, housing, employment and other services will be found to impinge directly on...teaching tasks. The implication is clear: educational priorities must be integrated into community development' (Halsey, 1977: 241). Similar conclusions are to be drawn from an OECD survey of integrated services for children and families at risk in 14 countries (OECD, 1995). It suggests that an important issue for us must be to get better coordination of services for disadvantaged families through effective inter-agency working. If disadvantage has multiple causes, tackling it requires strategies that bring together multiple agencies rather than expecting schools to seek their own salvation.

Paradoxically, at the same time as governments have tried to apply similar sets of policy solutions (e.g. quasi-markets, target-setting, etc.) across a whole range of social policy fields, they have also sought to downplay the relationship between those fields. Yet, it should be clear from what I have been saying that a major priority must be to provide incentives for effective inter-agency work to counter disadvantage. However, inter-agency working is not just a matter of ensuring greater efficiency in the delivery of public services, important as that is. It can also be done in such a way as to rebuild 'social capital' in disadvantaged communities.

Social capital has been defined as 'features of social organisation, such as trust, norms and networks, that can improve the efficiency of society by facilitating coordinated actions' (Putnam et al., 1993: 167). With regard to education, it refers to 'the set of resources that inhere in family relations and in community social organisation and that are useful for the cognitive or social development of a child or young person' (Coleman, 1994: 300). It is often linked to social class, but can be strong in less affluent groups and thereby, at least to a limited extent, counteract material disadvantage. The concept may therefore have some power to explain differential achievement between similarly materially disadvantaged groups.

The suggestion is that we need to rebuild the sort of trust and supportive social networks that have disappeared from many parts of modern societies (Putnam et al., 1993). Even if that argument can be exaggerated in the case of Britain as a whole, it does appear that the country is 'divided between a well-connected and active group of citizens and another whose associational life and involvement in politics is very limited' (Hall, 1997; 36). This has been exacerbated by recent policies that treat education as an individual consumer right rather than the responsibility of the whole community. So, even though substantial increases in material resources for disadvantaged groups may seem the most obvious and effective way of tackling inequalities, interventions that increase 'social capital' may also be useful in reducing risk, leading to consequent improvements in health, education and, indeed, economic prosperity in disadvantaged areas.

Research on social capital demonstrates its importance to educational achievement in communities as well as the potential role of education itself in building social capital. Policies that appear to have little to do with education, such as community development or the building of 'healthy alliances', may therefore contribute to the raising of achievement in schools. If disadvantage has multiple causes, tackling it requires strategies that bring together agencies that more usually work in isolation.

Support networks that increase 'social capital' may be useful in reducing risk, leading to consequent improvements in health, education and, indeed, economic prosperity. For example, an American study (Furstenberg and Hughes, 1995: 589) has suggested that social capital is a factor determining school staying-on rates among disadvantaged African-American young people in the USA. They further found that those with a higher level of social capital are less likely to be depressed, more likely to be in work, less likely to be teenage parents and more likely to have 'avoided serious trouble'. Another study (Fuchs and Reklis, 1994) concluded that the strength of parental relationships and the influence of other social networks are crucial in affecting children's 'readiness to learn' in pre-school contexts. Data from British birth cohort studies similarly suggest the importance of social capital in maximising educational potential. For example, Wadsworth's analyses (1996, 1997a, 1997b) indicate that parental interest in children's education impacts positively on educational outcomes, and on achievements and opportunities in adulthood, irrespective of social class. School effectiveness and improvement research similarly provides evidence that high levels of trust between headteacher and staff, between staff and pupils, and between home and school, are associated with beneficial outcomes. Moreover, in some circumstances, schools can help to build social capital in the wider community. Although participation in community and voluntary organisations is strongly differentiated by social class and education, women with low literacy and numeracy skills appear more likely to be involved in schools' PTA activities (6 per cent and 12 per cent respectively) than in any other local networks (Bynner and Parsons, 1997).

Early interventions seem likely to be particularly effective and Wadsworth argues that the 'chances of reduction of inequalities for any given generation will be greater the earlier attempts at reduction are begun. It is unlikely that inequalities can be easily or rapidly reduced, increasingly so as the individuals carry an accumulation of health potential which is hard to change' (1997b: 867). In view of this, it is interesting to note that early years educational initiatives tend to take a more holistic approach and recognise the importance of building social capital to a much greater extent than interventions in other phases.

Although still controversial, findings from two of the longest established US initiatives, High/Scope and Project Headstart, do seem to demonstrate impressive gains in health and social outcomes, particularly when pupils are compared with those staying at home or experiencing other forms of intervention (Schweinhart et al., 1993; Case et al., 1999). For example, only 6 per cent of those attending High/Scope – a programme based on a constructivist theory of child development – are reported as having received treatment for emotional difficulties during their primary or secondary education compared with 47 per cent of a group that had undergone an intervention involving direct instruction. Similarly, Headstart pupils have been reported as staying on at secondary school for an average of two years longer than those who did not attend a pre-school programme. They also seem to have experienced fewer teenage pregnancies, less delinquency, 'higher feelings of empowerment and a more positive attitude towards the education of their children' than the control group (Case et al., 1999). These direct and indirect social benefits suggest that every dollar invested in High/Scope-style pre-school education nets $7 in long-term savings on crime, health and other social expenditure (Schweinhart and Weikart, 1997).

We cannot just assume that findings from the US are necessarily applicable here. However, there is some evidence – from a range of initiatives piloted in the last twenty years – to suggest that good quality pre-school interventions can have positive effects in the UK too (see, for example, Jowett and Sylva, 1986; Athey, 1990; Shorrocks et al., 1992; Sylva and Wilshire, 1993). Interventions that focus on developing what has sometimes been called a 'readiness to learn' seem likely to bring particular benefits to disadvantaged children (Ball, 1994; Sylva and Wilshire, 1993). Support for parents can also be of vital importance in this context (Smith and Pugh, 1996). Although, over the years, many UK-based programmes have either been marginalised or abandoned before their outcomes could be properly evaluated, there is now a broad consensus among educationists, developmental psychologists, child and adolescent psychiatrists and researchers that high-quality interventions in the early years are one of the more effective ways of improving educational performance, self-esteem and emotional well-being. But that does not mean that later interventions, such as the current joint DfEE/DH 'Healthy Schools' initiative, cannot make a contribution.

Bryk et al. (1993) in the USA and recent studies here (Catholic Education Service, 1997, 1999; Grace, 1998) indicate that Catholic schools hold some important lessons for the education service as a whole. Such work suggests that the relative success of these institutions, particularly with some apparently disadvantaged groups, may be in part dependent upon strong levels of social capital within such schools and the communities that they serve (Willms, 1999). This conclusion is quite controversial in the USA, because Catholic schools there are private schools and the findings have been used to support the case for private education. The statistics have therefore been crawled over very intensively and it is clear that part of the apparent effect can be attributed to differences in the academic quality of the intake, different patterns of exclusion and differences in the academic programmes on offer. But there does still seem to be a residual effect of 'community', both in school and beyond school, which provides some support for the social capital thesis. More research is needed on the situation in the UK to establish the real causes of the apparently greater success of denominational schools here. This, in turn, might help determine how far non-religious forms of support and networking could help raise achievement in non-denominational schools.

New Labour Policies

So, bearing all these considerations in mind, how do current policies hold up? I shall also be discussing New Labour policies in Chapter 8, so will restrict my comments here to attempts to counter the effects of social disadvantage. Arguably, New Labour has sought to embrace elements of all the approaches tried to date, but its White Paper, *Excellence in Schools*, the subsequent School Standards and Framework Act 1998 and *Excellence in Cities* have placed a particular emphasis on school improvement strategies, backed by a strengthened accountability and support frameworks. Overall, whatever their benefits in particular schools, these policies have so far been relatively weak in respect of overcoming disadvantage and tackling inequalities. Certainly, there was initially a reluctance to confront the possibility that, even if its policies succeed in raising standards overall, they might exacerbate inequalities (Plewis, 1998). Indeed, New Labour's approach to target-setting has sometimes seemed to imply that it is possible to achieve equality of outcomes without addressing the impediments to equality of opportunity.

However, there are certain aspects of New Labour's wider policies that are rather more encouraging in this respect and reveal a degree of relational thinking and sociological credibility lacking in school-focused measures. The Social Exclusion Unit was launched by Tony Blair in December 1997 with a call for 'a Britain in which no-one is excluded from opportunity and the chance to develop their potential' and to make it 'our national purpose to tackle social division and inequality'. One of the functions of the Unit is to call departments to account if their policies do not seem to make a contribution to ending social exclusion. This could have a major effect on education policy, since some of the policies that remain in place from the previous regime have often had the effect of excluding rather than including, sometimes literally.

Wide-ranging interventions, such as Sure Start and Family Literacy, certainly look beyond the failures of schools for the causes of under-achievement. Schools matter, but so do families and communities and it is encouraging that the problems that many poor families encounter in providing appropriate educational support are at last being properly recognised, though the continuation of 'market principles' from some of the earlier policies may inadvertently be adding to the problems of schools and families in the poorest areas.

A recognition that there may be something in the social capital thesis and, more specifically, the evidence that denominational schools appear to have more success than others in raising the achievement of disadvantaged pupils, is part of the reason for New Labour's recent interest in increasing the number of faith-based schools in Britain (Penlington, 2001a). However, if the thesis does stand up to further scrutiny, the major policy issue facing the rest of the education service is surely whether and how equivalent forms of social capital can be constructed in non-denominational schools and among different populations. This constitutes a major challenge because communities that are high in social capital can often be socially and culturally exclusive rather than inclusive, as has been the case, for example, in Northern Ireland (Baron et al., 2000).

As I indicated earlier, a recognition of the necessity of positive discrimination is evident in one of the few specific education initiatives that signals a clear break with the policies of the Conservatives. The programme of Education Action Zones in areas with a mix of under-performing schools and the highest levels of disadvantage is intended to lever up standards and cut truancy rates. In theory, the policy could be responsive to some of the arguments I have been advocating here, particularly those about concentrating resources in areas of greatest disadvantage and building social capital through networks, partnerships and inter-agency collaboration. If they are to succeed, though, there will need to be a significant redistribution of resources into these areas and, as I suggested in Chapter 1, to involve all stakeholders more fully than appears to have been the case hitherto. At the same time, it will be important not to neglect the needs of disadvantaged groups beyond the zones. There will also need to be a clearer policy for forging links with other interventions both within and beyond education. Initially, Education Action Zones seemed to be conceived separately from Health Action Zones and Employment Zones, though there have since been promising moves to link at least some of them, while the Estates Renewal Initiative does clearly recognise the relationship between different aspects of social policy. Only such 'joined up' and holistic approaches are likely to be successful in sustaining, sharing and generalising effective school improvement strategies.

Two Aspects of Social Exclusion/Inclusion

Relational thinking requires that policies should not be purely concerned with the disadvantaged, since their disadvantage is relative to the advantage of others. Anthony Giddens (1998) points out that 'social exclusion' is a dual process, which operates at the 'top' as well as the 'bottom' of society, with the wealthy often excluding themselves voluntarily from state-provided services. As we all know, the ruling and upper middle classes in England have traditionally 'self-excluded' themselves from mainstream educational provision by their use of elite private education. The rapid growth of the middle classes since the Second World War has, however, not led to a similar growth in the size of that sector of education (Burchardt et al., 1999). So, although some of the newer fractions of the middle classes have made increasing use of private sector provision, others have had some success in 'colonising' particular parts of public education in ways that make it 'safe' for their own children. This may be part of the reason for the development of differentiated forms of state provision and for the emergence in some schools of what Halpin et al. (1997) have termed 'reinvented traditionalism'. Whatever the intention, some of these processes seem to have had the effect of excluding 'other people's children' from the best public provision.

Young (1999) demonstrates that these processes of exclusion 'at the top' and 'at the bottom' are interdependent in quite specific ways. He suggests that families with high enough incomes to afford alternatives avoid the state secondary schools in many inner London boroughs precisely because many of the pupils in such schools are from families who would on any criteria be classified as being among the excluded at the bottom. In some cases, this involves opting into the private sector, but even where better off families continue to use state schools at secondary level they often employ other mechanisms of 'exclusion at the top', such as moving house into the catchment areas of what they perceive to be the best state schools. In extreme cases, Young suggests, whole boroughs come to be regarded as unsafe for middle-class children. The falling quality of public services in large swathes of the inner cities is thus itself partly an outcome of the withdrawal of support for them by growing numbers of relatively advantaged people. School choice policies have often facilitated this strategic withdrawal of the middle classes, making it even more difficult for schools in those areas to succeed because, as Margaret Maden has indicated, it is important for such schools to have 'a "critical mass" of more engaged, broadly "pro-school" children to start with' (2001: 336).

Meanwhile, the sponsorship of a few 'meritorious' working-class children into thriving suburban schools of the middle-classes, whether public or private, helps to legitimate the system without threatening the critical mass of middle-class children in those schools. However, the broader problem of working-class failure is barely addressed by the existence of privileged routes for the few, whether assisted places, foundation schools or specialist schools, and, indeed, their very existence may serve to reduce the pressure for a more fundamental reform of provision. Individual meritocratic success stories of the sort that politicians like to cite as evidence of the success of their policies – such as their annual photoshots during the 1980s with some of the few unambiguously working-class pupils in the assisted places scheme – do not address the issue of structural inequalities and indeed can have the effect of legitimating them.

So does all this mean that education policy is unable to do anything effective to challenge these class differentials? We do know that, while similar social class effects can be detected in all countries (even those that deny it), the English case is an extreme one (Goldthorpe, 1996). So there are things that can be done to modify if not transform the prevailing patterns. We should therefore try to tackle the extent to which working-class children continue to be denied opportunities open to middle-class children on all fronts. While we certainly need to challenge the class basis of definitions of educational success and failure, and re-evaluate current in-school processes of differentiation, we should also seek to maximise the possibilities for working-class children to succeed on current definitions.

For example, evidence from the United States suggests that, while blanket class size reductions from above 30 to marginally below 30 may make no significant difference, targeted reductions to 15 for disadvantaged pupils do (Molnar et al., 1999). Perversely, the policy of reducing classes at Key Stage 1 to below 30, which was pursued by New Labour at the 1997 general election, probably benefited advantaged groups more than disadvantaged ones, as there were more classes over 30 in affluent areas than inner city ones. However, reducing class sizes to 15 in disadvantaged schools, which would effectively transfer resources away from more affluent areas, might be educationally desirable but might also prove an electoral liability.

It is certainly difficult for governments to pursue policies that seem to challenge middle-class privilege in the current political climate and New

Labour has generally been wary of doing so. It is understandable that policies have to speak particularly to the middle-class and aspiring middle-class voters who constitute the 'swing' vote that decides modern elections. Realistically, then, we have to find ways of working around this electoral logic while, if possible, limiting the opportunities for unjustified and unjustifiable middle-class advantage. The implication of seeing social *exclusion* as a dual process, as Giddens explicitly recognises, is that any programme for social *inclusion* must itself be a dual process. Strategies have to be developed for including 'the top' as well as 'the bottom' of society within the mainstream of public provision. Although it is not entirely clear how far this was intended, Excellence in Cities, the New Labour initiative to boost standards in inner-city state schools, may have the effect in some areas of retaining more middle-class children in such schools, as well as pursuing its more manifest aim of raising achievement among working-class groups. Getting the balance between the potentially positive effects of 'critical mass' and the dangers of middle-class 'colonisation' of both schools and the curriculum at the expense of working-class families will be difficult. Indeed, difficulties of this sort have already been commented upon in connection with the 'Gifted and Talented' strand of the initiative (Lucey and Reay, 2000). Nevertheless, Excellence in Cities does seem to herald, potentially at least, the beginnings of a more genuinely inclusive strategy.

Conclusion

As we have seen, many studies have drawn attention to the cumulative effects of low social class, poor educational achievement, reduced employment prospects, and poor physical and mental health. Notwithstanding Giddens' arguments in his most recent work (Giddens, 2000), there are not many families in Britain who are education rich but poor in other respects.

Although Secretary of State David Blunkett apparently dismissed his views as 'claptrap' (Pyke, 1997), Robinson's suggestion (1997) that an attack on poverty would be more effective in reducing educational inequalities than school-focused reforms, it is clear from our own research on the relationship between housing, health and education inequalities that, without a sustained attack on material poverty, any educational gains among disadvantaged groups are likely to be short-lived. Policies that are about building social capital are also important, but they are a necessary complement to rather than a substitute for policies that attack material poverty (Gamarnikow and Green, 1999). Education policy initiatives will have only limited success in overcoming social class differentials in achievement if they are not consciously articulated with policies that address those wider economic inequalities which, at least until recently, Giddens accepted 'had to be tackled at source' (Giddens, 1998).

The re-engineering of the educational system, so that disadvantaged groups can succeed, will certainly not be easy, nor will it be achieved by the education service alone. Probably the single most significant factor that currently distinguishes the most academically successful schools (even if not the most 'effective' ones in value-added terms) is that only a small proportion of their pupils come from disadvantaged homes. To that extent, policies that tackle poverty and related aspects of disadvantage at their roots are likely to be more successful than purely educational interventions in influencing overall patterns of educational inequality. Less social segregation in schooling could also contribute towards that end.

Society needs to be clearer about what schools can and cannot be expected to do and what support they need. The relationship between individuals, institutions and society is complex and blaming schools for the problems of society is both unfair and unproductive. It is certainly important for government, LEAs, diocesan authorities and school governors to work with teachers to set challenging goals but it is also important to be clear about the limits of school-based actions. Setting unrealistic goals and adopting a strategy of 'name and shame' will lead only to cynicism and a lowering of morale among those teachers at the heart of the struggle to raise the achievement of disadvantaged pupils. Teachers who choose to work in these schools – because they are committed to the disadvantaged – need this commitment recognised and supported. And they will need to work closely with other agencies if their work is to make a significant and sustained impact on relative levels of achievement among disadvantaged communities.

There is no one single factor that could serve to reverse long-standing patterns of disadvantage but neither should we regard them as an unchangeable fact of life. Schools can certainly make a difference, but they cannot buck social trends on their own. Michael Barber once caricatured such analyses as saying that 'schools make no difference' and that 'nothing can be done until after the revolution' (1997b: 21). That is not what I am saying, nor I hope, in saying it, will I be characterised as one of David Blunkett's hated 'energy-sappers and cynics' (*Times Educational Supplement*, 6 June 1997). What policy scholarship informed by sociological perspectives shows us is that, yes, schools can make a difference, but – as the author of the book I mentioned earlier (Thrupp, 1999) puts it – do 'let's be realistic!'

Further Reading

Maden, M. (ed.) (2001) *Success Against the Odds – Five Years On*. London: RoutledgeFalmer.

Mortimore, P. (1998) *The Road to Improvement: Reflections on School*

Effectiveness. Abingdon: Swets & Zeitlinger.

Thrupp, M. (1999) *Schools Making a Difference: Let's Be Realistic!* Buckingham: Open University Press.

Note

1. This chapter has been developed from a paper originally co-authored by Peter Mortimore.

8

New Labour, Education Policy and Educational Research

After the 1997 General Election, many people in Britain and abroad looked to a reforming New Labour government and its so-called 'Third Way' policies as providing a progressive alternative to the New Right agenda that had dominated education policy for the previous twenty years. This final chapter, on the present-day politics of education policy in England, considers how far those hopes are being borne out in practice and the extent to which a new agenda has now superseded the hegemony of the New Right reforms described earlier in this book. It also discusses New Labour's relationship to the academy and the use it makes of educational research in policy-making.

At times during the 1980s and 1990s, there was a tendency to regard neo-liberal education policies as the only possible response to globalisation and the situation confronting modern nation states. Yet, despite their popularity, the take-up of these reforms has been by no means universal, even if some unlikely countries have been experimenting with particular aspects of them (Green et al., 1999; Green, 2001). We should also remember that neither enhanced parental choice nor school autonomy is necessarily linked to a conservative agenda and that similar measures have, in other circumstances, been part of a more progressive package of policies. In Victoria, Australia and in New Zealand, for example, some of the reforms originated in a different tradition, but were subsequently incorporated into and thereby transformed by the rightist agenda (Whitty, Power and Halpin, 1998).

By the mid-1990s, there was anyway considerable public disquiet with the effects of the New Right agenda in many countries and this led to a return to power of centre left parties in some of them. The return of a New Labour government in Britain in May 1997 was welcomed by many people as heralding sharp changes in education policy. Education had certainly enjoyed a high profile during the election campaign, consistent with the declaration by Labour's leader, Tony Blair, that he would make his policy priorities 'education, education, and education'. New Labour's Third Way policies were also expected to point a new way forward for other countries that were becoming disillusioned with the prevailing neo-liberal ortho-doxy.

The New Labour Alternative

For those of us concerned about the damaging equity effects of the previous government's policies, there were certainly some positive aspects to the change of government. 'High quality education for the many rather than excellence for the few' was New Labour's promising slogan immediately following the 1997 election. The phasing out of the Assisted Places Scheme (one of the first policies of the Thatcher government, as mentioned in Chapter 3) seemed to suggest that privatisation and privilege would not be the favoured path of the new government. The fact that resources freed by the ending of the Assisted Places Scheme were to be used to reduce class sizes in infant schools suggested that – at least in principle – redistribution was back on the agenda. Another rhetorical shift represented specialist schools as a community resource rather than a privileged escape route for those attending them, implying that a degree of collective responsibility for the education of all children was to replace rampant competition among schools and parents. The new language was to be that of 'partnership', partnership between schools, partnership between schools and parents, partnership between schools and their LEAs, and even partnership between public and private sectors. Teachers were to be offered an enhanced sense of professionalism through a General Teaching Council, even if its powers were to be decidedly limited.

In practice, though, many of New Labour's changes to the Conservative agenda were largely cosmetic. In some of its manifestations, New Labour's so-called Third Way looked remarkably similar to quasi-markets. The central thrust of the policies was probably closer to that of the Conservative agenda than to Labour's traditional approach. Furthermore, some of the Conservative education policies most detested by the 'liberal educational establishment' were maintained and even strengthened under New Labour. The main elements of the reforms of the 1980s and early 1990s remained in place. Privatisation, in the sense of contracting out the provision of education services in both schools and LEAs, actually went further than the Thatcher and Major governments ever contemplated, while the relatively modest specialist schools initiatives of the Conservatives became a central plank of Labour policy (Tulloch, 2001).

In their personal and their political pronouncements, choice for both parents and schools was actively embraced by government ministers. Some of the comments made by Tony Blair on these matters were somewhat akin to Mrs Thatcher's notorious remark that there is 'no such thing as society, only individuals and families' (*Woman's Own*, 31 October 1987). There seemed little concern that, in a stratified society, school choice can too easily enable those who have the cultural resources to make the best choices to deny them to others. As former 'Old Labour' Minister, Roy Hattersley, once put it, it gives freedom to middle-class parents 'to talk their way into unfair advantage' (*Observer*, 15 January 1995).

Whatever its electoral appeal, this approach revealed a disturbing lack of sociological thinking in New Labour's education policy, and the lack of an appreciation that individual decisions have consequences for others. Yet, in some respects, the shift in Labour's approach was perhaps more understandable in sociological as well as electoral terms, being arguably a response to the sorts of changes to modern societies discussed in Chapter 5. Labour, in the words of Michael Barber (1997a: 175), first head of the Standards and Effectiveness Unit established at the Department for Education and Employment (DfEE) after the 1997 election, sought to 'link its traditional concern with equality with a new recognition of diversity'.

In doing so, however, New Labour seemed to accept the optimistic version of 'new times' in too uncritical a manner. In arguing that the key issue was 'standards not structures', the government tried to wish away a history in which the selection of children for unequal provision has been the dominant principle on which English secondary education has been organised. In the light of that history, any attempt to foster diverse forms of schooling within a broader commitment to comprehensive secondary education demands that serious attention be given to ways of preventing legitimate differences becoming unjust inequalities. However effective 'standards not structures' might have been as a soundbite, it should be clear from Chapter 7 that the quest to raise standards for all could not sensibly be divorced from issues of structure.

Furthermore, an approach based on diverse structures and common standards may have produced the worst of both worlds. In the context of 'high modernity', there may well be an argument for accepting a degree of diversity rather than opposing all schools which are not fully comprehensive in a conventional sense. But why apply that to structures and not to the nature of teaching and learning? The Blair government adopted an almost entirely conventional view of educational knowledge and displayed impatience with awkward sociological questions about its selective nature and social functions. Indeed, New Labour's notion of 'standards' was almost entirely unexamined. If anything, New Labour actually narrowed the curriculum and introduced prescriptive approaches to the teaching of literacy and numeracy. Thus, in its first term, New Labour took on board Conservative allegations of grey uniformity and pervading mediocrity, if not outright failure, in contemporary education but chose to deconstruct only certain elements.

If we look across the board, then, even New Labour's symbolic shifts were heavily constrained during its first term. Beyond that, the New Right settlement largely remained in place. We still had an admixture of state control and market forces, combining a National Curriculum and assessment system with quasi-markets based on local management, diversity and choice. There was, however, some re-centring of control, much of it involving a refinement of the sort of 'steering at a distance' that constitutes the new mode of regulation discussed in earlier chapters, although (as mentioned in Chapter 4) some of it was rather more reminiscent of the old style 'bureaucratic' state than Neave's 'evaluative' state (1988). At the same time, as indicated above, there was greater use of private sector contractors to revive failing schools and LEAs. To that extent, the balance within the policy repertoire was somewhat different, but its key elements remained the same.

The Comprehensive Question

Aspects of New Labour policy on class size, school improvement and educational disadvantage have been discussed in Chapter 7. Here I shall concentrate on its policies in relation to comprehensive education, one of Labour's flagship policies since the 1960s. Perhaps the clearest example of a shift away from Old Labour policies was the issue of the remaining 166 academically selective state grammar schools for 11–18 year olds, which had survived the policy of comprehensivisation and thrived during the Thatcher and Major administrations. There were even some people close to New Labour who argued that the party should formally rethink its opposition to academic selection, certainly at 14 if not 11. Interestingly, one of them, Will Hutton, has more recently revised his position and warned of the dangers of undermining comprehensive schooling (Hutton, 2001). But the government's own fudging of its position has probably been more damaging. David Blunkett claimed that grammar schools were numerically irrelevant. Yet even that is untrue in terms of their effects on particular local economies of schooling and, nationally, their symbolic significance remains tremendous.

Nevertheless, gone is the Old Labour certainty of 'If it is wrong to select and segregate children ... it must be wrong everywhere' expounded by Secretary of State, Ted Short, back in the 1960s (quoted in Kerckhoff et al., 1996: 34). Although the vast majority of secondary schools are now comprehensive at least in name, the continuing existence of some that are not leaves open the question of what precisely Labour does now stand for in secondary education. Rather than confront this, Labour went into the 1997 election with a pledge that the future of the remaining grammar schools would be decided by local parents. 'If there is no desire among local parents for a change in admissions policies, there will be no ballot and Conservative position. 'It cannot be right that good existing schools should be forcibly brought to an end, or that parents' freedom of choice should be so completely abolished,' said the Conservatives in 1958.

It might be argued that the change of heart was a welcome shift away from the centralised statism of Old Labour. But the actual proposals on the procedures for voting out grammar schools were not self-evidently democratic, since discussions about who should have the right to be heard were deliberately limited to avoid any potential embarrassment to the government. This retreat during the 1997 election from David Blunkett's 'watch my lips, no selection under Labour' speech at the 1995 Labour Party conference went even further while he was Secretary of State for Education and Employment. Between its initial White Paper *Excellence in Schools* and the School Standards and Framework Act 1998, the government conceded that partial selection could remain in schools at its present level where it already existed. One of the outcomes of all this is that, in the absence of credible value added analyses, selective schools figure strongly in the annual performance tables published by the news media with little attempt to explain that it would be surprising if they did not given their selective intakes.

Even if we were to accept that these are marginal issues, New Labour's central proposition that comprehensive schools should be different but equal is one which it is easy to make but difficult to deliver in the context of that polarisation of ethos, reputation and intake that, as indicated earlier, so many research studies have demonstrated (Whitty, 1997; Whitty, Power and Halpin, 1998). As we have seen, making notional choices available certainly does not appear to have benefited the poor to date, whatever choice advocates like Stephen Pollard (1995) in Britain or Terry Moe (1994) in America may like to believe. Differences in material and cultural resources, as well as knowledge of the differential likelihood of 'succeeding', have long contributed to class differences in participation and achievement within selective systems.

The covert forms of selection which have been uncovered by research on schools of choice by researchers like Stephen Ball, Sharon Gewirtz and Diane Reay (Gewirtz et al., 1995; Reay and Ball, 1998) may even produce greater inequalities, as socially advantaged parents learn to decipher the 'real' admissions criteria. Selection by interest and aptitude in music and dance is already being used by some schools to enhance the entry of academically able children from middle-class families. In this context, the government's energetic support for specialised schools, even with the new emphasis on their role within the local community, carries the danger of creating a hierarchy of schools based on the sorts of children who attend them. This certainly seems to have been the case with the early specialist schools (Gorard and Taylor, forthcoming), although advocates claim that this has not been the case with the later tranches (Taylor, 2001).

Almost equally disturbing to Old Labour critics was New Labour's decision to maintain elements of the Conservative distinction between LEA-maintained, voluntary-aided and grant-maintained status in the renamed forms of 'community', 'voluntary' and 'foundation' schools. Even though most grant-maintained schools identified themselves as compre-hensive schools, they were more likely than LEA-maintained schools to have sixth forms, relatively high proportions of middle-class pupils, and correspondingly low proportions of working-class and black pupils. Conservative efforts to present these schools as academically superior to others were intellectually dishonest in the absence of comparative data on free school meals, value-added performance and levels of exclusion, but they almost certainly influenced public perceptions. Labour's adoption of the terms 'community' and 'foundation' schools allowed the latter to trade upon their traditionalist image even after their advantages in terms of funding and control over admissions had been reduced (though not entirely removed).

Overall, there was a commitment to institutional diversity and choice even though some manifestations of this diversity undermined the integrity of others, the continuing existence of grammar schools alongside comprehensive ones being only the most obvious example. In practice, though, New Labour's commitment to diversity did not accommodate all-comers. Neighbourhood comprehensives were clearly off its agenda, while the meritocratic model of a comprehensive school ousted the egalitarian one. Yet the very diversity that New Labour embraced made it difficult to provide a level playing field on which a genuine meritocracy could flourish.

Prospects for the Second Term

With regard to issues of equity and inclusion, New Labour's first term policies thus seemed relatively weak. While New Labour has certainly been somewhat more sensitive than its Conservative predecessor to such issues, it is still in danger of becoming a failing government in this respect. Like failing schools, it therefore needs to be put under 'special measures'. In other words, to follow the metaphor through, our approach to New Labour's education policies should be something like its own avowed policy towards schools of 'challenge plus support'.

There is some evidence that Labour is susceptible and responsive to challenge on the issue of the achievement gap and is planning to make closing that gap a bigger priority in its second term. Indeed, the latest statistics suggest that the achievement gap may already have been narrowing in some respects. So, while the standards agenda has dominated the first term, some progress has already been made with inclusion. But, even if this proves to be a clear and consistent trend rather than a blip, there is an urgent need to increase the relative rate of improvement at the bottom end and make sure it extends to all disadvantaged pupils. It is significant that, to date, only certain minority ethnic groups have benefited from the improvement. It will be important to increase still further investment and support to schools in areas of multiple disadvantage and to provide it to disadvantaged groups in all schools.

How far is further pressure possible? As we saw in Chapter 7, the policy of reducing classes at Key Stage 1 to below 30 which was pursued by New Labour at the 1997 general election probably benefited advantaged groups more than disadvantaged ones. The significance of 'key aspirational middle-class groups' for New Labour, and their particular importance to education policy, has been clearly identified by McCaig (2000). Whether or not the class size policy in the 1997 election was designed to benefit that constituency, it has certainly had that effect. There was an even clearer electoral basis for the apparent retreat of New Labour from the party's historic commitment to comprehensive schools, its ambivalent stance towards the abolition of grammar schools and its enthusiastic adoption of the Conservative's specialist schools policy during its first term (Edwards and Whitty, 1997; Edwards et al., 1999).

The grammar school issue has not gone away. Despite a ballot defeat in Ripon, comprehensive school campaigners are continuing to pursue their cause (Chitty and Simon, 2001). Meanwhile, John Marks (2001) has recently reiterated claims that academic standards have suffered in England as a result of comprehensivisation. When I co-authored a review of the evidence in 1999 (Crook et al., 1999), we came to the conclusion that overall there was too little robust evidence on either side of the argument to come to a definitive judgement on this. Our best judgement was that comprehensive schools had improved the academic performance of most groups of children, though were perhaps not as effective with the most able. David Jesson's more recent, though controversial, analyses of the data (Jesson, 2000) suggest that even that last caveat may now need revision. What our pamphlet did not make explicit enough in my view was that improvement in academic achievement is not the only, or necessarily the most important, justification for comprehensive schools. Comprehensive schools are even more important to the social inclusion agenda than to the standards agenda.

With regard to specialist schools, the Green Paper issued just before the 2001 general election (DfEE, 2001), made clear that specialisation and diversity in secondary education remain a key New Labour priority. It laid out ambitious plans for substantial increases in the numbers of specialist schools and faith-based schools. These are justified partly by research by Jesson (Jesson and Taylor, 1999) suggesting superior academic performance and rates of improvement on the part of the existing specialist schools. However, the dangers of covert selection, hierarchy and confusion I alluded to above remain (Smithers, 2001). The chances of creating a hierarchy of schools are, of course, likely to be increased if there are significant differences in funding levels. We do not so far have robust enough research evidence to tell us whether the claimed better performance of specialist schools results from anything other than their enhanced funding, but it is likely to make them increasingly attractive to some parents (Edwards and Eavis, 2001; West et al., 2000).

More positively, in terms of social inclusion, advocates like Penlington (2001b) of the Social Market Foundation suggest that the hidden intent behind New Labour's version of the specialist schools policy is to bring a critical mass of middle-class children into schools in disadvantaged areas without driving out their traditional clientele, which rather as I suggested in Chapter 7 might be a positive, though not necessarily intended, consequence of Excellence in Cities if it is handled carefully. Penlington (2001c) argues, apparently without irony, that 'it is unusual to base an entire policy on spin'. But in this case, she says, 'spin may be the most effective way to achieve two antagonistic goals: encouraging the middle classes to use the state sector while simultaneously raising levels of provision in Britain's worst-off communities' (2001c: 9).

With New Labour's continuing adherence to a policy of diversity and specialist schools, advocates of more conventional forms of comprehensive education will have to decide the extent to which it is appropriate for schools to have distinctive characters. At times, they have seemed to defend existing comprehensive schools on the grounds that they are not in practice as uniform as the prime minister appears to believe, while at the same time resisting his attempts to give them more distinctive missions. But however much diversity is allowed to develop, it will be important to insist on rebuilding a comprehensive *system* of secondary education and curbing the excesses of quasi-markets. In order to avoid diversity producing a hierarchical two-tier system, all schools in an area will need to work together in the interests of optimum provision for all pupils. Genuine collegiality among schools would be much easier if they were all put on the same legal and budgetary footing, whatever private and voluntary sector partners are involved in their governance. There also needs to be much stronger regulation of a common admissions system. The present code of practice, while an advance on Conservative arrangements, has failed to stamp out current abuses. Status, budgets and admissions should thus be key areas for further action if the standards and inclusion agendas are to be successfully brought together.

Then there are other aspects of inclusion that need be pursued in New Labour's second term. As mentioned in Chapter 7, Education Action Zones have provided some examples of multi-agency working between education, health and welfare services to tackle multiple disadvantage. However, I suspect the New Community Schools initiative in Scotland, drawing on the experience of full-service schools in the USA, may well provide a better model for comprehensive school-based services and greater community involvement in schools (Campbell et al., 2000).

We also need to recognise that local education authorities as we know them may not necessarily be the only, or even the best, way of either governing or managing education. But we do not need to conclude from that that privatisation is the only viable alternative. The USA is often quoted as a precedent for the involvement of for-profit companies in running schools and school districts, but there are many examples of such initiatives going wrong there (Molnar, 1996). Furthermore, the policy is one with long-term dangers. While private companies see rich pickings in taking over the management of LEAs and schools at the present time, they are drawing in people from the public sector to help them take advantage of it. But, if public sector capacity is undermined by this, what will happen when the private sector moves on to seek easier profits elsewhere? This is one reason why we need to maintain a strong public sector and, to that extent, the notion that it is what works rather than who does it that matters may in the longer term prove to be misguided even in pragmatic terms, let alone in principle.

It would certainly be unwise to undermine democratic accountability or the public service ethos at the centre of our education system, however many new partners may be involved in its delivery at any one time. For this reason, I would like to see as much emphasis placed on new forms of governance as on new forms of management. In theory at least, New Labour is open to a range of models of governance, provided they raise achievement. With a renewed emphasis on collaboration rather than competition, there ought to be scope for experimentation with new forms of governance with or without LEAs and new ways of addressing the democratic deficit in education through, for example, joint governing bodies and local education forums. Such arrangements could also help the process of developing social capital in disadvantaged areas. This, as I have argued earlier, is an aspect of Education Action Zones that has been relatively neglected to date.

It is also surely time to pursue the question of the comprehensive curriculum, one of the key challenges for the comprehensive school identified by David Hargreaves in the 1980s (Hargreaves, 1982). The government has indicated that secondary education will be a priority in its second term. At Key Stage 4, the issue still seems to be seen largely in terms of academic or vocational routes, or the balance between them, rather than an overall and inclusive reconceptualisation of the curriculum. But Key Stage 3 is likely to be a major priority where current thinking is rather less clear. Here, in my view, Labour should look to enrich rather than narrow the curriculum, while making it more challenging. Raising literacy and numeracy scores by gradgrindery, or by neglecting areas such as the arts, are not in anyone's long-term interests, least of all the socially disadvantaged. Reforms in some countries have managed to tackle the unquestionable need to raise standards in the basics without sacrificing breadth. Labour's introduction of education for citizenship into the National Curriculum and various initiatives in personal and social education are part of the answer but do not adequately address the concerns about the curriculum identified in Chapters 2 and 6. The government will need to take things further, perhaps by picking up on some of David Hargreaves' recent ideas on encouraging creativity and innovation (Hargreaves, 2000).

Not surprisingly, teachers also report similar needs to exercise creativity and innovation. Labour governments of the 1960s and 1970s managed to harness the commitment and creativity of teachers for the comprehensive project. Even allowing for a bit of 'golden age-ism' in this view, the contrast with the present situation is certainly stark. This government has still to win the hearts and minds of teachers, except in so far as they fear the alternative even more. The formation of the General Teaching Council had considerable symbolic value for the teaching profession, while the resignation of Chris Woodhead from Ofsted certainly raised morale for a time. But there is still a long way to go before teachers feel that this government trusts and values their professionalism.

Transferring some additional functions to the GTC would help, but the character and public image of teaching needs serious attention. Although pay is a key factor in the current teacher supply crisis, too many people are put off teaching because it is seen as a bureaucratic rather than a creative profession. This, together with the attraction of the new media industries, may be one of the reasons for an unprecedented shortage of English teachers in some parts of London. As with pupils, incentives and rewards for creativity and innovation will need to be put back into the system to give teaching some of the excitement as well as the challenge that many of us felt when we started teaching in comprehensive schools in the 1960s. In doing this, however, we must make sure that schools in disadvantaged areas are able to recruit and retain at least their fair share of talented teachers. There is a danger that reducing regulation for successful schools, while welcome in many respects, could unwittingly make schools in more challenging circumstances even less attractive to the most creative teachers and thus contribute to their further decline.

More generally, extending the powers of central government over 'failing' schools and LEAs may make it difficult to close the achievement gap if 'successful' schools are meanwhile left to their own devices to maximise their advantages in the marketplace for funding, students and teachers. The balance between consumer rights and citizen rights, which was discussed in Chapter 5, is therefore a key issue that will confront New Labour education policy in its second term.

New Labour and the Academy

These are all issues that could be tackled through closer collaboration between policy-makers and researchers in informing the democratic process. The recruitment in 1997 of Michael Barber, a professor at the Institute of Education, to head the Standards and Effectiveness Unit, and the early influence of the school effectiveness and school improvement movement, might have been expected to herald a close connection between New Labour and educational researchers and a renewed commitment to interchange. Prior to the election, some people had even predicted a return to a Golden Age of the 1960s, when sociologists such as A. H. Halsey were listened to by the then Labour government of Harold Wilson, although even that era probably looks better in retrospect than it felt at the time.

Yet, even if the picture of a close connection between research and policy-making in the 1960s is partly an 'imagined past', the climate under New Labour became decidedly difficult quite quickly after the 1997 election. In debates about the flagship EAZ policy, it was striking how little New Labour had learned or knew – or perhaps even cared – about the past. There was little evidence that it has looked systematically at the positive and negative lessons that might be learned from Educational Priority Areas (EPAs), Urban Development Corporations or City Technology Colleges, all of which had some echoes in Education Action Zones and all of which had generated research studies that could have yielded important lessons for the new initiative. And, although policy advisers now used the new language of social capital and social inclusion, some of the early snags must have seemed all too familiar to those who were involved in the various community development projects of the 1960s and 1970s. There was also an apparent lack of attention to relevant research evidence from abroad. Plewis (1998) pointed out that lessons from the experience of France and the Netherlands had similarly been ignored in the planning of Education Action Zones. And, although Molnar's damning critique of the role of business in schools in the USA (Molnar, 1996) has been cited in the British press, the government still seems willing to contemplate working with some of the same players.

At the same time, there seemed for a while to be a growing tendency on the part of New Labour to ignore or even demonise the so-called educational establishment almost as much its Tory predecessor had done. In commenting on some of my own work (Whitty, Power and Halpin, 1998), Wilby suggested that research findings demonstrating that policies of devolution and choice often had damaging equity effects were not familiar ground to politicians (Wilby, 1998). Yet that was certainly not true of some of their advisers and, indeed, some of the research that was now systematically ignored or derided by Labour ministers had actually been quoted by them with approval in Opposition.

Plewis and Goldstein (1998), whose assistance had also been courted by Labour in Opposition, suggested that the government was ignoring research that called into question the viability of some of its key policies on standards and targets. As we saw in Chapter 7, David Blunkett dismissed as 'claptrap' the views of Peter Robinson (1997) of the London School of Economics, when he argued that an attack on poverty might do more for levels of literacy and numeracy than the government's targets (quoted in Pyke, 1997). Meanwhile, a government spokesperson had ridiculed parts of the Institute of Education's response to the schools White Paper (DfEE, 1997) as 'utterly absurd and farcical' (cited in Hackett, 1997), an outburst that provoked its then Director, Peter Mortimore – who many would have regarded as a natural ally of New Labour – to a spirited defence of the role of universities and public intellectuals in a liberal democracy (Mortimore, 1998a).

New Labour often seemed to demand that academics were either with the government 100 per cent or they were regarded as against it. David Blunkett's words to head teachers in June 1997 that 'if you are not with us then step aside for there is no room in the education service for those who do not believe we can do better' was also reflected in the attitude towards academic commentators. Even to suggest that current policies might not be the best way of doing better, or asking whether we are clear what we mean by doing better, was too often regarded as treachery. But if, for example, some of New Labour's policies appeared to be serving the demands of new middle-class voters at the expense of the truly disadvantaged, then it was surely important to be able to say so without being accused of being 'energy-sappers' who 'erode the enthusiasm and the hope that currently exists' (*Times Educational Supplement*, 6 June 1997).

Towards the end of his time as Secretary of State, David Blunkett (2000) gave a more measured assessment of the role of academics in relation to government in a lecture to the Economic and Social Research Council entitled 'Influence or Irrelevance: Can Social Science Improve Government?' In it, he talked about the relationship between government and the social science research community and took a number of his examples of both good and bad practice from education research. Coming after a long period of tension between governments and education researchers in the aftermath of the Tooley and Hillage Reports (Tooley and Darby, 1998; Hillage et al., 1998), it included a welcome acknowledgement of a need for the government to 'move forward' in its relationship with researchers and expressed a willingness on his part to give 'serious consideration' to 'difficult' findings. On the other hand, he reiterated his frustration that too many researchers chose to address issues other than those 'which are central and directly relevant to the policy debate' and instead were 'driven by ideology paraded as intellectual inquiry or critique, setting out with the sole aim of collecting evidence that will prove a policy wrong rather than genuinely seeking to evaluate or interpret impact' (2000: 2).

The government had meanwhile established a National Education Research Forum to bring together the various stakeholders in education research and its consultation paper, issued in 2000 (NERF, 2000), has reignited concerns that the government has a very limited and instrumental view of research, constituting a commitment to what Grace (1991) terms policy science rather than policy scholarship. As the Institute of Education said in its response to the paper, it is based on a simplistic notion of education research – one which makes a clear distinction between education research and other kinds of research and one which suggests that policies and practices will be improved by a straightforward application of research findings. This position glosses over the diverse and contested nature of education research and ignores the political and professional imperatives that can often militate against policy-makers and practitioners 'applying' research findings to their practices. It also, incidentally, overlooks the benefits to be gained from the large volume of research being undertaken into education systems and developments in other countries.

By no means all worthwhile and rigorous research into education is directly linked to current policy and practice. Some studies focus on historical aspects, philosophical underpinnings, changing modes of policy-making or the constitution of education systems. This kind of research may be of little immediate relevance to those engaged in current policy and practice, but it does provide important insights into contemporary society and addresses enduring social issues that are often lost sight of in more applied research. Furthermore, a lot of this research is relevant to practice and it would be unfortunate to disregard it just because it did not set out directly or even indirectly to influence practice. Although 'fundamental' research is mentioned in the introduction to the consultation paper, it subsequently disappears and the focus is on issues of current concerns, such as teacher recruitment and retention and the impact of ICT.

In a stinging attack on the NERF consultation paper, Stephen Ball (2001) says that the paper regards research as 'about providing accounts of "what works" for unselfconscious classroom drones to implement' and that 'it portends an absolute standardization of research purposes, procedures, reporting and dissemination' (2001: 266–7). Whether or not this is entirely fair, such a reaction suggests that relations between researchers and New Labour policy-makers remain tense.

Nevertheless, there are some more hopeful signs. The government has established a number of policy-oriented research centres in universities, including three in which the Institute of Education is involved. In its commitment to evidence-informed policy and practice and disseminating research knowledge to teachers, it seems to have pulled back from the notion that only the findings of randomised control trials on the medical model produce useful evidence. This is welcome because professional educators do not just need to know 'what works' in education, they also need to understand why something works and, equally important, why it works in some contexts and not in others. We also need opportunities to consider whether the activity is a worthwhile endeavour in the first place.

These are crucial aspects of professional literacy, which higher education is particularly well suited to support through research and teaching. For example, in the MOTE project, discussed in Chapter 4, we found that, while student teachers who had undertaken mainly school-based training were as well versed as others in which approaches to teaching reading worked best, they were much less confident than those with college-based support that they knew why. If professionals are to be required to make judgements and adapt to changing circumstances, they will need to have this degree of professional literacy. Otherwise Ball's 'unconscious classroom drones' jibe may just turn out to be true, although it is highly unlikely that the teaching profession itself will succumb to such a technicist project notwithstanding the trends in that direction identified in Chapter 4.

Universities are particularly well-placed to foster broader research literacy because we are not constrained by one particular definition of what counts as research and we can pursue lines of enquiry which are often marginalised in agencies that are thoroughly embedded in an instrumentalist or pragmatic culture. A healthy education service, as part of a healthy democracy, requires that we, like Mannheim, should resist the growing tendency 'to discuss problems of organisation rather than ideas, techniques rather than aims' (1951: 199). And we need to recognise, like Clarke, that educational theory and educational policy that ignore wider social issues 'will be not only blind but positively harmful'.

Conclusion

While contemporary societies demand greater degrees of diversity and choice than may have been the case in the past, New Labour's plans for diversity and choice within a broadly comprehensive system do not yet provide enough systemic safeguards to stop that becoming a selective system in all but name. However, there are tensions within New Labour education policy and, although there has been a retreat from traditional approaches to comprehensive education, there are still important things that can be done to further the cause of equity and social inclusion.

Doing so will involve taking cognisance of the insights of both the old and the new sociologies of education and combining what Nancy Fraser (1997) terms the politics of recognition with the politics of redistribution. Within the academy and the wider community, we need both to challenge the social basis of prevailing definitions of educational success and failure where they are inappropriate, while supporting disadvantaged children in their efforts to succeed on current definitions. While this may appear utopian, I would argue that, unlike policies that merely do the one thing or the other, it is – in the terms outlined in Chapter 1 – a 'realistic' utopian project that is consistent with the pursuit of democracy and social justice.

Further Reading

Chitty, Clyde and Simon, Brian (eds) (2001) *Promoting Comprehensive Education in the 21st Century*. Stoke-on-Trent: Trentham Books.

Crook, David, Power, Sally and Whitty, Geoff (1999) *The Grammar School Question*. London: Institute of Education.

Docking, Jim (ed.) (2000) *New Labour's Policies for Schools: Raising the Standard?* London: David Fulton.

References

Adams, A. and Tulasiewicz, W. (1995) *The Crisis in Teacher Education: a European Concern?* London: Falmer Press.

Adler, M. (1993a) *An Alternative Approach to Parental Choice.* London: National Commission on Education.

Adler, M. (1993b) Parental choice and the enhancement of children's interests, in Munn, P. (ed.), *Parents and Schools: Customers, Managers or Partners?* London: Routledge.

Alexander, T. (2001) *Citizenship Schools.* London: Campaign for Learning.

Angus, L. (1993) The sociology of school effectiveness, *British Journal of Sociology of Education*, Vol. 14, no. 3, pp. 333–45.

Anyon, J. (1995) Race, social class, and educational reform in an inner-city school, *Teachers College Record*, Vol. 97, no. 1, pp. 69–94.

Apple, M. W. (1986) *Teachers and Texts.* New York: Routledge & Kegan Paul.

Apple, M. W. (1996) *Cultural Politics and Education.* Buckingham: Open University Press.

Apple, M. W. (2001) *Educating the Right Way: Markets, Standards, God and Equality.* New York: RoutledgeFalmer.

Apple, M. W. and Beane, J. (eds) (1996) *Democratic Schools.* Buckingham: Open University Press.

Apple, M. W. and Whitty, G. (1999) Structuring the postmodern in education, in Hill, D. and Cole, M. (eds), *Postmodernism and Education.* London: Tufnell Press.

Arnot, M. (1998) Respondent: 'Distressed worlds': social justice through educational transformations, in Carlson, D. and Apple, M. W. (eds), *Power/Knowledge/Pedagogy: The Meaning of Democratic Education in Unsettling Times.* Boulder, CO: Westview Press.

Arnot, M., David, M., and Weiner, G. (1998) *Closing the Gender Gap: Postwar Education and Social Change.* Cambridge: Polity Press.

Arnott, M., Bullock, A., and Thomas, H. (1992) *Consequences of Local Management: An Assessment by Head Teachers.* Paper presented at the ERA Research Network, University of Warwick, 12 February.

Arnove, R. (1996) *Neo-liberal Education Policies in Latin America: Arguments in Favor and Against.* Paper presented at the Comparative and International

Education Society, Williamsburg, 6–10 March.

Aronowitz, S. (1992) *The Politics of Identity*. New York: Routledge.

Ascher, C. and Power, S. (2000) *The Hub and the Rim: Policy Paradoxes in Charter Schools and Grant Maintained Schools*. Paper presented to the Annual Meeting of the American Educational Research Association, New Orleans, 24–30 April.

Athey, C. (1990) *Extending Thought in Young Children*. London: Paul Chapman.

Atkinson, D. (1994) *Radical Urban Solutions*. London: Cassell.

Atkinson, D. (1997) *Towards Self-governing Schools*. London: The Institute of Economic Affairs.

Bailey, L. (1995) The correspondence principle and the 1988 Education Reform Act, *British Journal of Sociology of Education*, Vol. 16, no. 4, pp. 479–94.

Ball, S. J. (1990) *Politics and Policy Making: Explorations in Policy Sociology*. London: Routledge.

Ball, S. J. (1994) *Education Reform: A Critical and Post-structural Approach*. Buckingham: Open University Press.

Ball, S. J. (1995) Intellectuals or technicians? The urgent role of theory in educational studies, *British Journal of Educational Studies*, Vol. 43, no. 3, pp. 255–71.

Ball, S. J. (2001) 'You've been NERFed!' Dumbing down the academy: National Educational Research Forum: 'a national strategy – consultation paper': a brief and bilious response, *Journal of Education Policy*, Vol. 16, no. 3, pp. 265–68.

Bandura, A. (1995) Exercise of personal and collective efficacy in changing societies, in Bandura, A. (ed.), *Self Efficacy in Changing Societies*. Cambridge: Cambridge University Press.

Barber, M. (1996a) Education reform, management approaches and teacher unions, in Leithwood, K., Chapman, J., Corson, D., Hallinger, P. and Hart, A. (eds), *International Handbook of Educational Leadership and Administration*. Dordrecht: Kluwer Academic Publishers.

Barber, M. (1996b) *The Learning Game: Arguments for an Education Revolution*. London: Gollancz.

Barber, M. (1997a) Educational leadership and the global paradox, in Mortimore, P. and Little, V. (eds), *Living Education*. London: Paul Chapman.

Barber, M. (1997b) Hoddle showed us how the White Paper can succeed, *Times Educational Supplement*, 7 November, p. 21.

Barnett, R. (1994) *The Limits to Competence: Knowledge, Higher Education and Society*. Buckingham: Open University Press.

Baron, S., Field, J. and Schuller, T. (eds) (2000) *Social Capital: Critical Perspectives*. Oxford: Oxford University Press.

Bartlett, W. (1993) Quasi-markets and educational reforms, in Le Grand, J. and Bartlett, W. (eds), *Quasi-Markets and Social Policy*. London: Macmillan.

Bassuk, E. and Rosenberg, L. (1988) Why does family homelessness occur? A case-control study, *American Journal of Public Health*, Vol. 78, pp. 783–8.

Beck, U., Giddens, A. and Lash, S. (1994) *Reflexive Modernization*. Cambridge: Polity Press.

Benzeval, M., Judge, K. and Whitehead, M. (1995) *Tackling Inequalities in Health*. London: King's Fund.

Bernstein, B. (1971) On the classification and framing of educational knowledge, in Young, M. F. D. (ed.), *Knowledge and Control*. London: Collier Macmillan.

Bernstein, B. (1977). *Class, Codes and Control*, Vol. 3, 2nd edn. London: Routledge & Kegan Paul.

Bernstein, B. (1981) Codes, modalities and the process of cultural reproduction: a model, *Language and Society*, Vol. 10, pp. 327–63.

Bernstein, B. (1990) *The Structuring of Pedagogic Discourse*. London: Routledge.

Bernstein, B. (1996) *Pedagogy, Symbolic Control and Identity*. London: Taylor & Francis.

Bernstein, B. (1997) Official knowledge and pedagogic identities, in Nilsson, I. and Lundahl, L. (eds), *Teachers, Curriculum and Policy*. Umea, Sweden: Umea University.

Bernstein, B. (2000) *Pedagogy, Symbolic Control and Identity: Theory, Research, Critique*, rev. edn. Lanham, MD: Rowman & Littlefield.

Berrill, M. (1994) A view from the crossroads, *Cambridge Journal of Education*, Vol. 24, no. 1, pp. 113–16.

Blackburne, L. (1988) Peers back policy on open enrolment, *Times Educational Supplement*, 13 May.

Blackmore, J. (1990) School-based decision making and trade unions, in Chapman, J. (ed.), *School-based Decision-making and Management*. London: Falmer Press.

Blackmore, J. (1995) Breaking out from a masculinist politics of education, in Limerick, B. and Lingard, B. (eds), *Gender and Changing Education Management*. Rydalmer, NSW: Hodder Education.

Blackmore, J. (1996) *The Re-gendering and Restructuring of Educational Work*. Paper presented to the Ninth World Congress of Comparative Education Societies, Sydney, Australia, 1–6 July.

Blank, R. (1990) Educational effects of magnet high schools, in Clune, W. H. and Witte, J. F. (eds), *Choice and Control in American Education*, Vol. 2. New York: Falmer Press.

Blunkett, D. (2000) *Influence or Irrelevance: Can Social Science Improve Government?* ESRC Lecture Speech by the Secretary of State, Department for Education and Employment, London.

BMA (1999) *Growing Up in Britain*. London: BMA Board of Science and Education, BMA Science Department.

Bottery, M. (1996) The challenge to professionals from the new public management: implications for the teaching profession, *Oxford Review of Education*, vol. 22, pp. 179–97.

Bourdieu, P. and Passeron, J. (1977) *Reproduction in Education, Culture and Society*. London: Sage.

Bowe, R., Ball, S. J. and Gewirtz, S. (1994) Captured by the discourse: issues and concerns in researching parental choice, *British Journal of Sociology of Education*, Vol. 15, no. 1, pp. 63–78.

Bowe, R., Ball, S. J. and Gold, A. (1992) *Reforming Education and Changing Schools*. London: Routledge.

Bowles, S. and Gintis, H. (1976) *Schooling in Capitalist America*. London: Routledge & Kegan Paul.

Boyne, R. and Rattansi, A. (eds) (1990) *Postmodernism and Society*. London: Macmillan.

Boyson, R. (1990) Review of T. Edwards, J. Fitz and G. Whitty, The State and Private Education, *Times Higher Education Supplement*, 18 May.

Bramstedt, E. K. and Gerth, H. (1951) A note on the work of Karl Mannheim, in *K. Mannheim, Freedom, Power and Democratic Planning*. London: Routledge.

Brighouse, T. (1996) *A Question of Standards: the Need for a Local Democratic Voice*. London: Politeia.

Brown, P., Halsey, A. H., Lauder, H. and Wells, A. (1997) The transformation of education and society: an introduction, in Halsey, A. H., Lauder, H., Brown, P. and Wells, A. (eds), *Education: Culture, Economy and Society*. Oxford: Oxford University Press.

Bruner, J. and Haste, H. (1987) *Making Sense*. London: Methuen.

Bryk, A. S., Lee, V. E. and Holland, P. B. (1993) *Catholic Schools and the Common Good*. Cambridge, MA: Harvard University Press.

Bullock, A. and Thomas, H. (1994) *The Impact of Local Management of Schools: Final Report*. Birmingham: University of Birmingham.

Bullock, A. and Thomas, H. (1997) *Schools at the Centre? A Study of Decentralisation*. London: Routledge.

Burchardt, T., Hills, J. and Propper, C. (1999) *Private Welfare and Public Policy*. York: Joseph Rowntree Foundation.

Bush, T., Coleman, M. and Glover, D. (1993) *Managing Autonomous Schools*. London: Paul Chapman.

Bynner, J. and Parsons, S. (1997) *It Doesn't Get Any Better: The Impact of Poor Basic Skills on the Lives of 37 Year Olds*. London: Basic Skills Agency.

Callinicos, A. (1989) *Against Post Modernism: A Marxist Critique*. Cambridge: Polity Press.

Campbell, C., Gillborn, D., Lunt, I., Robertson, P., Sammons, P., Vincent, C., Warren, S. and Whitty, G. (eds) (2000) *Review of Developments in Inclusive Schooling*. Report to the Scottish Executive Education Department, Institute of Education.

Case, R., Griffin, S. and Kelly, W. M. (1999) Socioeconomic gradients in mathematical ability and their responsiveness to intervention during early childhood, in Keating, D. P. and Hertzman, C. (eds), *Developmental Health and the Wealth of Nations: Social, Biological and Educational Dynamics*. New York: Guilford.

Cassidy, S (2000) Market proves a divisive force, *Times Educational Supplement*, 17 March, p. 28.

Catholic Education Service (1997) *A Struggle for Excellence: Catholic Secondary Schools in Urban Poverty Areas*. Report of a consultation 1995–1997 for the Department for Catholic Education and Formation of the Catholic Bishops' Conference of England and Wales, April 1997.

Catholic Education Service (1999) *Foundations for Excellence: Catholic Primary Schools in Urban Poverty Areas*. Report of a consultation 1997–1999 for the Department for Catholic Education and Formation of the Catholic Bishops' Conference of England and Wales, July 1999.

Chapman, J. (1988) Teacher participation in the decision making of schools, *Journal of Educational Administration*, Vol. 26, no. 1, pp. 39–72.

Chitty, C. and Simon, B. (eds) (2001) *Promoting Comprehensive Education in the 21st Century*. Stoke-on-Trent: Trentham Books.

Chubb, J. and Moe, T. (1990) *Politics, Markets and America's Schools*. Washington, DC: Brookings Institution.

Chubb, J. and Moe, T. (1992) *A Lesson in School Reform from Great Britain*. Washington, DC: Brookings Institution.

Clarke, F. (1967) Karl Mannheim at the Institute of Education, Appendix B of Mitchell, F. W., *Sir Fred Clarke: Master-Teacher 1880–1952*. London: Longmans.

Clewell, B. C. and Joy, M. F. (1990) *Choice in Montclair, New Jersey*. Princeton, NJ: ETS.

Codd, J. A. (1996) *Professionalism versus Managerialism in New Zealand Schools*. Paper presented at the British Educational Research Association Annual Meeting, University of Lancaster, 12–15 September.

Cohen, J. and Rogers, J. (1995) *Associations and Democracy*. London: Verso.

Coleman, J. S. (1994) *Foundations of Social Theory*. Cambridge, MA: Belknap Press.

Coleman, J. S., Hoffer, T. and Kilgore, S. (1982) *High School Achievement: Public, Catholic and Private Schools*. New York: Basic Books.

Connell, R. W. (1993) *Schools and Social Justice*. Toronto: Our Schools/Our Selves Education Foundation.

Cookson, P. W. (1994) *School Choice: The Struggle for the Soul of American Education*. New Haven, CT: Yale University Press.

Cooper, B. (1992) Testing National Curriculum mathematics, *Curriculum Journal*, Vol. 3, p. 3.

Crane, H. (1990) *Speaking from Experience – Working with Homeless Families*. London: Bayswater Hotel Homeless Project.

Crook, D., Power, S. and Whitty, G. (1999) *The Grammar School Question.* London: Institute of Education.

Dale, R. (1989) *The State and Education Policy.* Milton Keynes: Open University.

Dale, R. (1990) The Thatcherite project in education: the case of the city technology colleges, *Critical Social Policy*, Vol. 9, no. 3, pp. 4–19.

Dale, R. (1994) *Neo-liberal and neo-Schumpeterian Approaches to Education.* Paper presented at the conference on Education, Democracy and Reform, University of Auckland, 13–14 August.

Davies, B. (1994) Durkheim and the sociology of education in Britain. *British Journal of Sociology of Education*, Vol. 15, no. 1, pp. 3–25.

Davies, C. (1996) The sociology of professions and the profession of gender, *Sociology*, Vol. 30, pp. 661–78.

Demaine, J. (ed.) (1999) *Education Policy and Contemporary Politics.* London: Macmillan.

Demaine, J. (ed.) (2001) *Sociology of Education Today.* Basingstoke: Palgrave.

Dennehy, A., Smith, L. and Harker, P. (1997) Not to be ignored: young people, poverty and health, in Walker, A. and Walker, C. (eds), *Britain Divided: the Growth of Social Exclusion in the 1980s and 1990s.* London: Child Poverty Action Group.

Department for Education (1992a) *Choice and Diversity: a New Framework for Schools.* London: HMSO.

Department for Education (1992b) *Initial Teacher Training (Secondary Phase) Circular 9/92.* London: DfE.

Department for Education and Employment. (DfEE) (1997a) *Excellence in Schools.* London: Stationery Office.

Department for Education and Employment (DfEE) (1998) *The Learning Age: a Renaissance for a New Britain.* London: Stationery Office.

Department for Education and Employment (DfEE) (2001). *Schools: Building on Success: Raising Standards, Promoting Diversity, Achieving Results.* London: HMSO.

Dickson, M., Halpin, D., Power, S., Telford, D. and Whitty, G. (2001) Education Action Zones and democratic participation, *School Leadership and Management*, Vol. 21, no. 2, pp. 169–81.

Docking, J. (ed.) (2000) *New Labour's Policies for Schools: Raising the Standard?* London: David Fulton.

Domanico, R. J. (1990) *Restructuring New York City's Public Schools: The Case for Public School Choice*, Education Policy Paper #3, New York, Manhattan Institute for Policy Research.

Donald, J. (1990) Interesting times, *Critical Social Policy*, Vol. 9, no. 3, pp. 39–55.

Douglas, R. (1993) *Unfinished Business.* Auckland: Random House.

Driver, R., Guesne, E. and Tiberghien, A. (1985) *Children's Ideas in Science.* Milton Keynes: Open University Press.

Edwards, R. (1992) Co-ordination, fragmentation and definitions of need: the new Under Fives Initiative and homeless families, *Children and Society*, Vol. 6, no. 4, pp. 336–52.

Edwards, T. and Eavis, P. (2001) Specialisation with tiers, in Chitty, C. and Simon, B. (eds), *Promoting Comprehensive Education in the 21st Century*. London: Trentham Books.

Edwards, T. and Whitty, G. (1997) Specialisation and selection in secondary education, *Oxford Review of Education*, Vol. 23, no. 5, pp. 5–15.

Edwards, T., Fitz, J. and Whitty, G. (1989) *The State and Private Education: an Evaluation of the Assisted Places Scheme*. London: Falmer Press.

Edwards, T., Whitty, G. and Power, S. (1999) Moving back from comprehensive education? in Demaine, J. (ed.), *Education Policy and Contemporary Politics*. London: Macmillan.

Eraut, M. (1994) *Developing Professional Knowledge and Competence*. London: Falmer Press.

Etzioni, A. (1969) (ed.) *The Semi-Professions and their Organization: Teachers, Nurses, Social Workers*. London: Collier-Macmillan.

Eurostat (1997) Children in poverty: Britain tops the European league, *The Guardian*, 28 April.

Featherstone, M. (1995) *Undoing Culture: Globalization, Postmodernism and Identity*. London: Sage.

Feintuck, M. (1994) *Accountability and Choice in Schooling*. Buckingham: Open University Press.

Fiske, E. B. and Ladd, H. F. (2000) *When Schools Compete: A Cautionary Tale*. Washington DC: Brookings Institute.

Fitz, J., Halpin, D. and Power, S. (1993) *Grant Maintained Schools: Education in the Marketplace*. London: Kogan Page.

Flax, J. (1987) Postmodernism and gender relations in feminist theory, *Signs*, Vol. 12, no. 4, pp. 621–43.

Fliegel, S. with Macguire, J. (1990) *Miracle in East Harlem: The Fight for Choice in Public Education*. New York: Random House.

Floud, J. (1959) Karl Mannheim, in Judges, A. V. (ed.), *The Function of Teaching*. London: Faber & Faber.

Floud, J. (1977) *Functions, Purposes and Powers in Education*. Paper presented at the Charles Gittins Memorial Lecture, Swansea, University College of Swansea.

Fowler, G. (1992) Non-hierarchical teaching: an ideological analysis of cultural transmission and a model for use in post-compulsory education and training. Unpublished PhD thesis, University of Nottingham.

Fowler, M. (1993) *Factors Influencing Choice of Secondary Schools*. Christchurch: University of Canterbury.

Fraser, N. (1997) *Justice Interrupts: Critical Reflections on the 'Postsocialist Condition'*. New York: Routledge.

Freidson, E. (1983) The theory of professions: state of the art, in Dingwall, R. and Lewis, P. (eds), *The Sociology of the Professions*. London: Macmillan.

Fuchs, V. R. and Reklis, D. M. (1994) *Mathematical Achievement in Eighth Grade: Interstate and Racial Differences*, NBER Working Paper 4784. Stanford, CA: NBER.

Furley, A. (1989) *A Bad Start in Life – Children, Health and Housing*. London: Shelter.

Furlong, J., Barton, L., Miles, S., Whiting, C. and Whitty, G. (2000) *Teacher Education in Transition: Re-forming Professionalism?* Buckingham: Open University Press.

Furstenberg, F. F. Jr and Hughes, M. E. (1995) Social capital and successful development among at-risk youth, *Journal of Marriage and the Family*, Vol. 57, pp. 580–92.

Gamarnikow, E. and Green, A. (1999) Developing social capital: possibilities and limitations in education, in Hayton, A. (ed.), *Tackling Disaffection and Social Exclusion*. London: Kogan Page.

Gamble, A. (1988) *The Free Economy and the Strong State*. London: Macmillan.

Geddes, M. (1996) *Extending Democratic Practice in Local Government*. Greenwich: Campaign for Local Democracy.

Gewirtz, S. (1998) *Education Policy in Urban Places: Making Sense of Action Zones*. Paper presented to Social Policy Annual Conference, University of Lincolnshire and Humberside, 14–16 July.

Gewirtz, S. (1999) Education Action Zones: emblems of the Third Way? in Dean, H. and Woods, R. (eds), *Social Policy Review 11*. Luton: Social Policy Association.

Gewirtz, S., Ball, S. J. and Bowe, R. (1992) *Parents, Privilege and the Educational Marketplace*. Paper presented at the Annual Conference of the British Educational Research Association, Stirling, 31 August.

Gewirtz, S., Ball, S. J. and Bowe, R. (1995). *Markets, Choice and Equity*. Buckingham: Open University Press.

Gibbons, M., Limoges, C., Nowotny, H., Schwartzman, S., Scott, P. and Trow, M. (1994) *The New Production of Knowledge*. London: Sage.

Gibson, A. and Asthana, S. (1998) School performance, school effectiveness and the 1997 White Paper, *Oxford Review of Education*, Vol. 24, no. 2, pp. 195–210.

Giddens, A. (1984) *The Constitution of Society*. Cambridge: Polity Press.

Giddens, A. (1994a) *Beyond Left and Right: The Future of Radical Politics*. Cambridge: Polity Press.

Giddens, A. (1994b) Living in a post-traditional society, in Beck, U., Giddens, A. and Lash, S. (eds), *Reflexive Modernization*. Cambridge: Polity Press.

Giddens, A. (1998) *The Third Way: The Renewal of Social Democracy*. Cambridge: Polity Press.

Giddens, A. (2000) *The Third Way and its Critics*. Cambridge: Polity Press.

Gillborn, D. and Youdell, D. (2000) *Rationing Education: Policy, Practice, Reform and Equity*. Buckingham: Open University Press.

Ginsburg, M. B. (1997) Professionalism or politics as a model for educators' engagement with/in communities, *Journal of Education Policy*, Vol. 12, nos. 1/2, pp. 5–12.

Giroux, H. and McLaren, P. (1992) America 2000 and the politics of erasure: democracy and cultural difference under siege, *International Journal of Educational Reform*, Vol. 1, no. 2, pp. 99–109.

Glatter, R., Woods, P. and Bagley, C. (1997) Diversity, differentiation and hierarchy: School choice and parental preference, in Glatter, R., Woods, P. A. and Bagley, C. (eds), *Choice and Diversity in Schooling: Perspectives and Prospects*. London: Routledge.

Gleeson, D. and Whitty, G. (1976) *Developments in Social Studies Teaching*. London: Open Books.

Glennerster, H. (1991) Quasi-markets for education? *Economic Journal*, Vol. 101, 1268–76.

Goldhaber, D. D. (1996) Public and private high schools: is school choice an answer to the productivity problem? *Economics of Education Review*, Vol. 15, pp. 93–109.

Goldhaber, D. D. (1999) School choice: an examination of the empirical evidence on achievement, parental decision-making, and equity, *Educational Researcher*, Vol. 28, no. 9, pp. 16–25.

Goldthorpe, J. H. (1996) Class analysis and the reorientation of class theory: the case of persisting differentials in educational attainment, *British Journal of Sociology*, Vol. 47, no. 3, pp. 482–505.

Goodson, I. (1983) *School Subjects and Curriculum Change*. London: Croom Helm.

Goodson, I. (ed.) (1985) *Social Histories of the Secondary Curriculum*. Lewes: Falmer Press.

Gorard, S. and Fitz, J. (1998a) Under starter's orders: the established market, the Cardiff Study and the Smithfield Project, *International Studies in Sociology of Education*, Vol. 8, no. 3, pp. 299–314.

Gorard, S. and Fitz, J. (1998b) The more things change...the missing impact of marketisation? *British Journal of Sociology of Education*, Vol. 19, no. 3, pp. 365–76.

Gorard, S. and Taylor, C. (forthcoming) The composition of specialist schools in England: track record and future prospects.

Gordon, L. (1992) Educational reform in New Zealand: contesting the role of the teacher, *International Studies in Sociology of Education*, Vol. 2, no. 1, pp. 23–42.

Gordon, L. (1994) 'Rich' and 'poor' schools in Aotearoa, *New Zealand Journal of Educational Studies*, Vol. 29, no. 2, pp. 113–25.

Gordon, L. and Wilson, K. (1992) Teacher unions in New Zealand, in Cooper, B. (ed.), *Labor Relations in Education*. Westport, CT: Greenwood Press.

Grace, G. (1984) *Education in the City*. London: Routledge & Kegan Paul.

Grace, G. (1991) Welfare Labourism versus the New Right: the struggle in New Zealand's education policy, *International Studies in Sociology of Education*, Vol. 1, no. 1, pp. 25–42.

Grace, G. (1995) *School Leadership: Beyond Education Management: an Essay in Policy Scholarship*. London: Falmer Press.

Grace, G. (1996) *Urban Education and the Culture of Contentment*. Paper presented at King's College London, 3 December.

Grace, G. (1998) Realising the mission: Catholic approaches to school effectiveness, in Slee, R., Weiner, G. and Tomlinson, S. (eds), *School Effectiveness for Whom? Challenges to School Effectiveness and School Improvement Movements*. London: Falmer Press.

Grace, G. (forthcoming) *Catholic Schools: Mission, Markets and Morality*. London: RoutledgeFalmer.

Gray, J. (1998) *The Contribution of Educational Research to School Improvement*. Inaugural Professorial Lecture, Institute of Education, University of London.

Gray, J. (2001) Introduction: building for improvement and sustaining change in schools serving disadvantaged communities, in Maden, M. (ed.), *Success Against the Odds – Five Years On: Revisiting Schools in Disadvantaged Areas*. London: RoutledgeFalmer.

Green, A. (1990) *Education and State Formation*. London: Macmillan.

Green, A. (1994) Postmodernism and state education, *Journal of Education Policy*, Vol. 9, no. 1, pp. 67–84.

Green, A. (1997) *Education, Globalisation and the Nation State*. London: Macmillan.

Green, A. (2001) Education at a crossroads, *Perspectives – The Japan Foundation Newsletter*. London, Issue 3, March.

Green, A., Wolf, A. and Leney, T. (1999) *Convergence and Divergence in European Education and Training Systems*. Bedford Way Paper, Institute of Education, London.

Greene, J. and Peterson, P. (1996) School choice data rescued from bad science, *Wall Street Journal*, 14 August.

Greene, J., Peterson, P. and Du, J. (1998) School choice in Milwaukee: a randomized experiment, in Peterson, P. E. and Hassel, B. C. (eds), *Learning from School Choice*. Washington, DC: Brookings Institution.

Hackett, G. (1997) Researchers' warning on national targets, *Times Educational Supplement*, 25 October, p. 3.

Hall, P. A. (1997) Social capital: a fragile asset, in Christie, I. and Perry, H. (eds), *The Wealth and Poverty of Networks: Tackling Social Exclusion*.

London: Demos.

Hall, S. (1991) The local and the global: globalization and ethnicity, in King, A. D. (ed.), *Culture, Globalization and the World-System*. London: Macmillan.

Hallgarten, J. and Watling, R. (2001) Zones of contention, *Parliamentary Brief*, Vol. 7, no. 2, pp. 44–5.

Halpin, D. (1999) Democracy, inclusive schooling and the politics of education, *International Journal of Inclusive Education*, Vol. 3, no. 3, pp. 225–38.

Halpin, D., Power, S. and Fitz, J. (1997) Opting into the past? Grant maintained schools and the reinvention of tradition, in Glatter, R., Woods, P. and Bagley, C. (eds), *Choice and Diversity in Schooling: Perspectives and Prospects*. London: Routledge.

Halsey, A. H. (ed.) (1972) *Educational Priority, EPA Problems and Policies, 1*. London: HMSO.

Halsey, A. H. (1977) Government against poverty in school and community, in Cosin, B. R., Dale, I. R., Esland, G. M., Mackinnon, D. and Swift, D. F. (eds), *School and Society: a Sociological Reader*. London: Routledge & Kegan Paul.

Halsey, A. H., Lauder, H., Brown, P. and Stuart Wells, A. (eds) (1997) *Education: Culture, Economy, Society*. Oxford: Oxford University Press.

Hammersley, M. (1996) Post mortem or post modern? Some reflections on British sociology of education, *British Journal of Educational Studies*, Vol. 44, no. 4, pp. 394–406.

Hanlon, G. (1998) Professionalism as enterprise: service class politics and the redefinition of professionalism, *Sociology*, Vol. 32, no. 1, pp. 43–63.

Hargreaves, A. (1994) *Changing Teachers, Changing Times: Teachers' Work and Culture in the Postmodern Age*. London: Cassell.

Hargreaves, D. (1982) *The Challenge for the Comprehensive School*. London: Routledge & Kegan Paul.

Hargreaves, D. (1994) *The Mosaic of Learning: Schools and Teachers for the Next Century*. London: Demos.

Hargreaves, D. (2000) *Towards Education for Innovation: How Can Education Systems Meet the Demands of a Knowledge Society?* Presentation at the Institute of Education, London, 22 November.

Harris, K. (1993) Power to the people? Local management of schools, *Education Links*, Vol. 45, pp. 4–8.

Harris, S. (1993) CEG post National Curriculum: What future? *Careers Education and Guidance*, October, pp. 2–3.

Harty, S. (1994) 'Pied Piper revisited', in Bridges, D. and McLaughlin, T. H. (eds), *Education and the Market Place*. London: Falmer Press.

Harvey, D. (1989) *The Condition of Postmodernity: an Enquiry into the Origins of Cultural Change*. Oxford: Basil Blackwell.

Hatcher, R. (1994) Market relationships and the management of teachers,

British Journal of Sociology of Education, Vol. 15, no. 1, pp. 41–62.

Hatcher, R. (1996) The limitations of the new social democratic agendas, in Hatcher, R. and Jones, K. (eds), *Education after the Conservatives*. Stoke-on-Trent: Trentham Books.

Hayek, F. A. (1944) *The Road to Serfdom*. London: Routledge.

Health Education Authority (HEA) (1992) *Health Education Policies in Schools*. London: Health Education Authority.

Henig, J. R. (1994) *Rethinking School Choice: Limits of the Market Metaphor*. Princeton, NJ: Princeton University Press.

Hickox, M. (1995) Situating vocationalism, *British Journal of Sociology of Education*, Vol. 16, no. 2, pp. 153–63.

Hickox, M. and Moore, R. (1992) Education and post-Fordism: a new correspondence, in Brown, P. and Lauder, H. (eds), *Education for Economic Survival: from Fordism to post-Fordism*. London: Routledge.

Hill, D., McLaren, P., Cole, M. and Rikowski, G. (eds) (1999) *Postmodernism in Educational Theory*. London: Tufnell Press.

Hill, P. T., Foster, G. E. and Gendler, T. (1990) *High Schools with Character*. Santa Monica, CA: Rand.

Hillage, J., Pearson, R., Anderson, A. and Tamkin, P. (1998) *Excellence in Research in Schools*. Sudbury: DfEE.

Hillgate Group (1987) *The Reform of British Education*. London: Claridge Press.

Hirst, P. Q. and Thompson, G. (1996) *Globalization in Question: the International Economy and the Possibilities of Governance*. Cambridge: Polity Press.

HMCI (1998) *Secondary Education 1993–97: A Review of Secondary Schools in England*. London: Office for Standards in Education.

Holland, J. (1981) Social class and changes in orientation to meaning, *Sociology*, Vol. 15, no. 1, pp. 1–18.

Howarth, V. (1987) *Survey of Families in Bed and Breakfast Hotels*. London: Thomas Coram Foundation for Children.

Hoyle, E. (1962) *Karl Mannheim and the Education of an Elite*. Unpublished MA dissertation, University of London.

Hoyle, E. (1964) The elite concept in Karl Mannheim's sociology of education, *Sociological Review*, Vol. 12, pp. 55–71.

Hoyle, E. (1974) Professionality, professionalism and control in teaching, *London Education Review*, Vol. 3, no. 2, pp. 13–19.

Hoyle, E. and John, P. D. (1995) *Professional Knowledge and Professional Practice*. London: Cassell.

Hutton, W. (2001) *Times Educational Supplement*, 16 February.

Jesson, D. (2000) The comparative evaluation of GCSE value-added performance by type of school and LEA. Available on http://www.york.ac.uk/depts/econ/rc/cperm.htm

Jesson, D. and Taylor, C (1999) *Value-Added in Specialist Schools*. London:

Technology Colleges Trust.

Jessop, B., Bonnett, K., Bromley, S. and Ling, T. (1987) Popular capitalism, flexible accumulation and left strategy, *New Left Review*, Vol. 165, pp. 104–23.

Johnson, S. M. and Landman, J. (2000) 'Sometimes bureaucracy has its charms': the working conditions of teachers in deregulated schools, *Teachers College Record*, Vol. 102, no. 1, p. 85.

Jones, L. and Moore, R. (1993) Education, competence and the control of expertise, *British Journal of Sociology of Education*, Vol. 14, pp. 385–97.

Jowett, S. and Sylva, K. (1986) Does kind of pre-school matter? *Educational Research*, Vol. 25, no. 1, pp. 21–31.

Keddie, N. (1971) Classroom knowledge, in Young, M. F. D. (ed.), *Knowledge and Control*. London: Collier Macmillan.

Kenway, J. (1993) Marketing education in the postmodern age, *Journal of Education Policy*, Vol. 8, no. 1, pp. 105–22.

Kenway, J. with Bigum, C., Fitzclarence, L. and Collier, J. (1998) Pulp fictions? Education, markets and the information superhighway, in Carlson, D. and Apple, M. (eds), *Power/Knowledge/Pedagogy*. Boulder, CO: Westview Press.

Kerckhoff, A., Fogelman, K., Crook, D. and Reeder, D. (1996) *Going Comprehensive in England and Wales*. London: Woburn Press.

Kettler, D. and Meja, V. (1995) *Karl Mannheim and the Crisis of Liberalism: The Secret of These New Times*. New Brunswick, NJ: Transaction Publishers.

Kettler, D., Meja, V. and Stehr, N. (1984) *Karl Mannheim*. Chichester: Ellis Horwood Limited.

Knight, J., Bartlett, L. and McWilliam, E. (eds) (1993) *Unfinished Business: Reshaping the Teacher Education Industry for the 1990s*. Rockhampton: University of Central Queensland.

Kozol, J. (1988) *Rachel and Her Children: Homeless Families in America*. New York: Crown.

Kritzman, L. D. (ed.) (1988). *Foucault: Politics/Philosophy/Culture*. New York: Routledge.

Kudomi, Y. (1996). Karl Mannheim in Britain: an interim research report, *Hitotsubashi Journal of Social Studies*, Vol. 28, no. 2, pp. 43–56.

Ladwig, J. (1994) For whom this reform? Outlining educational policy as a social field. *British Journal of Sociology of Education*, Vol. 15, no. 3, pp. 341–63.

Lander, G. (1983) *Corporatist Ideologies and Education: the Case of the Business Education Council*. Unpublished PhD thesis, University of London.

Landman, M. and Ozga, J. (1995) Teacher education policy in England, in Ginsburg, M. and Lindsay, B. (eds), *The Political Dimension in Teacher Education: Comparative Perspectives on Policy Formation, Socialization and Society*. London: Falmer Press.

Lash, S. (1990) *Sociology of Postmodernism*. London: Routledge.

Lauder, H., Jamieson, I. and Wikeley, F. (1998) Models of effective schools: limits and capabilities, in Slee, R., Tomlinson, S. and Weiner, G. (eds), *School Effectiveness for Whom?* London: Falmer Press.

Lauder, H., Hughes, D., Waslander, S., Thrupp, M., McGlinn, J., Newton, S. and Dupuis, A. (1994) *The Creation of Market Competition for Education in New Zealand.* Smithfield Project, Victoria University of Wellington.

Lauder, H., Hughes, D., Watson S., Waslander, S., Thrupp, M., Strathdee, R., Simiyu, I., Dupuis, A., Mcglinn, J. and Hamlin, J. (1999) *Trading in Futures: Why Markets in Education Don't Work.* Buckingham: Open University Press.

Lawlor, S. (1990) *Teachers Mistaught: Training in Theories or Education in Subjects?* London: Centre for Policy Studies.

Lawton, D. (1975) *Class, Culture and the Curriculum.* London: Routledge.

Lee, V. E. and Bryk, A. S. (1993) Science or policy argument? in Rassell, E. and Rothstein, R. (eds), *School Choice: Examining the Evidence.* Washington, DC: Economic Policy Institute.

Le Grand, J. (1997). Knights, knaves or pawns? Human behaviour and social policy. *Journal of Social Policy,* Vol. 26, pp. 149–64.

Le Grand, J. and Bartlett, W. (eds) (1993) *Quasi-Markets and Social Policy.* London: Macmillan.

Levacic, R. (1995) *Local Management of Schools: Analysis and Practice.* Milton Keynes: Open University Press.

Levacic, R. and Hardman, J. (1999) The performance of grant maintained schools in England: an experiment in autonomy, *Journal of Education Policy,* Vol. 14, no. 2, pp. 185–212.

Literacy Task Force (1997) *A Reading Revolution: How We Can Teach Every Child to Read Well.* London: Literacy Task Force.

Loader, C. (1985) *The Intellectual Development of Karl Mannheim.* Cambridge: Cambridge University Press.

Lucey, H. and Reay, D. (2000) *Carrying the Beacon of Excellence: Pupil Performance, Gender and Social Class.* Mimeograph, School of Education, King's College, London.

Mac an Ghaill (1992) Teachers' work: curriculum restructuring, culture, power and comprehensive schooling, *British Journal of Sociology of Education,* Vol. 13, no. 2, pp. 177–200.

McCaig, C. (2000) New Labour and education, education, education, in Smith, M. and Ludlum, S. (eds), *New Labour in Government.* London: Macmillan.

McKenzie, J. (1995) The process of excluding 'education' from the 'public sphere', in Edgell, S. et al. (eds), *Debating the Future of the Public Sphere.* Aldershot: Avebury.

McKenzie, D. (1999) The clouded trail: ten years of public education post-Picot, in Thrupp, M. (ed.), *A Decade of Reform in New Zealand: Where to Now?* Waikato: University of Waikato.

Maclure, S. (1993) Fight this tooth and nail, *Times Educational Supplement*, 18 June.

Maden, M. (ed.) (2001) *Success Against the Odds Five Years On*. London, RoutledgeFalmer.

Maden, M. and Hillman, J. (1996) Lessons in success, in National Commission on Education (ed.), *Success Against the Odds*. London: Routledge.

Mahoney, P. and Hextall, I. (2000) *Reconstructing Teaching: Standards, Performance and Accountability*. London: RoutledgeFalmer.

Mannheim, K. (1936) *Ideology and Utopia: An Introduction to the Sociology of Knowledge*. London: Kegan Paul.

Mannheim, K. (1940) *Man and Society in an Age of Reconstruction*. London: Kegan Paul.

Mannheim, K. (1943) *Diagnosis of Our Time: Wartime Essays of a Sociologist*. London: Kegan Paul.

Mannheim, K. (1951) *Freedom, Power and Democratic Planning*. London: Routledge & Kegan Paul.

Mannheim, K. (1957) *Systematic Sociology: an Introduction to the Study of Society*. London: Routledge & Kegan Paul.

Mannheim, K. and Stewart, W. A. C. (1962) *An Introduction to the Sociology of Education*. London: Routledge & Kegan Paul.

Marks, J. (2001) *The Betrayed Generation: Standards in British Schools 1950–2000*. London: Centre for Policy Studies.

Marquand, D. (1995) Flagging fortunes, *The Guardian*, 13 July.

Marren, E. and Levacic, R. (1994) Senior management, classroom teacher and governor responses to local management of schools, *Educational Management and Administration*, Vol. 22, no. 1, pp. 39–53.

Meja, V. and Kettler, D. (1993) Introduction, in Wolff, K. H. (ed.), *From Karl Mannheim*. New Brunswick, NJ: Transaction Publishers.

Millerson, G. (1964) *The Qualifying Association*. London: Routledge & Kegan Paul.

Mills, C. W. (1961) *The Sociological Imagination*. Harmondsworth: Penguin.

Moe, T. (1994) The British battle for choice, in Billingsley, K. L. (ed.), *Voices on Choice: The Education Reform Debate*. San Francisco: Pacific Institute for Public Policy.

Molnar, A. (1996) *Giving Kids the Business: the Commercialization of America's Schools*. Boulder, CO: Westview Press.

Molnar, A., Smith, P., Zahorik, J., Palmer, A., Halbach, A. and Ehrle, K. (1999) Evaluating the SAGE programme, *Educational Evaluation and Policy Analysis Journal*, Special Issue: Class size – issues and findings, Vol. 21, no. 2 pp. 165–79.

Montgomery, S. M. and Schoon, I. (1997) Health and health behaviour, in Bynner, J., Ferri, E. and Shepherd, P. (eds), *Twentysomething in the 1990s: Getting On, Getting By, Getting Nowhere*. Aldershot: Ashgate.

Moore, D. and Davenport, S. (1990) School choice: the new improved sorting machine, in Boyd, W. and Walberg, H. (eds), *Choice in Education*. Berkeley, CA: McCutchan.

Mortimore, J. and Blackstone, T. (1982) *Education and Disadvantage*. London: Heinemann.

Mortimore, P. (1996) *Partnership and Co-operation in School Improvement*. Paper presented at the Association for Teacher Education in Europe Conference, Glasgow, Scotland, September.

Mortimore, P. (1998a) Neither whingers nor pessimists, *Times Educational Supplement*, 31 October, p. 19.

Mortimore, P. (1998b) *The Road to Improvement: Reflections on School Effectiveness*. Abingdon: Swets & Zeitlinger.

Mortimore, P. and Whitty, G. (1997) *Can School Improvement Overcome the Effects of Disadvantage?* London: Institute of Education.

Mortimore, P., Sammons, P., Stoll, L., Lewis, D. and Ecob, R. (1988a) *School Matters: The Junior Years*. London: Open Books.

Mortimore, P., Sammons, P., Stoll, L., Lewis, D. and Ecob, R. (1988b) The effects of school membership on students' educational outcomes, *Research Papers in Education*, Vol. 3, no. 1, pp. 3–26.

Morton, S. (1988) *Homeless Families in Manchester*. Faculty of Community Medicine, University of Manchester.

Mouffe, C. (1989) Toward a radical democratic citizenship, *Democratic Left*, Vol. 17, no. 2, pp. 6–7.

Mouffe, C. (ed.) (1992) *Dimensions of Radical Democracy: Pluralism, Citizenship, Democracy*. London: Verso.

Mumby, D. and Stohl, C. (1991) Power and discourse in organization studies: absence and the dialectic of control, *Discourse and Society*, Vol. 28, no. 2, pp. 313–32.

Nash, R. and Harker, R. (1998) *Making Progress: Adding Value in Secondary Education*. Palmerston North: ERDC Press.

National Child Development Study (1972) *From Birth to Seven: The Second Report of the National Child Development Study (1958 Cohort)*. London: Longman/National Children's Bureau.

National Children's Bureau (1987) *Investing in the Future – Child Health Ten Years After the Court Report*. London: National Children's Bureau.

National Commission on Education (1996) *Success Against the Odds: Effective Schools in Disadvantaged Areas*. London: Routledge.

National Consumer Council (NCC) (1996) *Sponsorship in Schools*. London: National Consumer Council.

National Curriculum Council (NCC) (1990a) *Curriculum Guidance 3: The Whole Curriculum*. York: National Curriculum Council.

National Curriculum Council (NCC) (1990b) *Curriculum Guidance 5: Health Education*. York: National Curriculum Council.

Neave, G. (1988) On the cultivation of quality, efficiency and enterprise: an overview of recent trends in higher education in Western Europe, 1968–1988, *European Journal of Education*, Vol. 23, nos. 1/2, pp. 7–23.

NERF (2000) *A National Strategy*. Consultation paper issued by the National Forum for Educational Research. London: NERF.

Noden, P. (2000) Rediscovering the impact of marketisation: dimensions of social segregation in England's secondary schools, 1994–99, *British Journal of Sociology of Education*, pp. 371–90.

Noss, R. (1990) The National Curriculum and Mathematics: a case of divide and rule? in Noss, R. and Dowling, P. (eds), *Mathematics versus the National Curriculum*. Lewes: Falmer Press.

OECD (1994) *School: A Matter of Choice*. Paris: OECD/CERI.

OECD (1995) *Our Children at Risk*. Paris: OECD.

OERI (Office of Educational Research and Improvement) (1997) *A Study of Charter Schools: First Year Executive Report Summary*. Washington, DC: US Department of Education.

Ozga, J. (1990) Policy research and policy theory, *Journal of Education Policy*, Vol. 5, no. 4, pp. 359–62.

Ozga, J. (2000) *Doing Research in Educational Settings: Contested Terrain*. Buckingham: Open University Press.

Penlington, G. (2001a) Why New Labour found itself converted to Church schools, *Parliamentary Brief*, Vol. 7, no. 2, pp. 42–3.

Penlington, G. (2001b) Wooing the middle class into inner city schools, *Parliamentary Brief*, Vol. 7, no. 8, pp. 9–10.

Penlington, G. (2001c) Specialist spin that works, *Times Educational Supplement*, 10 August, p. 9.

Peterson, P. E. (1998) School choice: a report card, in Peterson, P. E. and Hassel, B. C. (eds), *Learning from School Choice*. Washington, DC: Brookings Institution.

Phillips, M. (1996) Inspectors only come under fire when they say schools are doing badly. No-one complains about their methods when the results are good, *Observer*, 27 October.

Plank, S., Schiller, K. S., Schneider, B. and Coleman, J. S. (1993) Effects of choice in education, in Rassell, E. and Rothstein, R. (eds), *School Choice: Examining the Evidence*. Washington, DC: Economic Policy Institute.

Plant, R. (1990) Citizenship and rights, in *Citizenship and Rights in Thatcher's Britain: Two Views*. London: Institute of Economic Affairs.

Plewis, I. (1997) Letter, *Times Educational Supplement*, 9 May.

Plewis, I. (1998) Inequalities, targets and zones, *New Economy*, Vol. 5, no. 2, pp. 104–8.

Plewis, I. and Goldstein, H. (1998) Excellence in schools – a failure of standards, *British Journal of Curriculum and Assessment*, Vol. 8, no. 1, pp. 17–20.

Pollard, S. (1995) *Schools, Selection and the Left*. London: Social Market Foundation.

Power, S., Fitz, J. and Halpin, D. (1994) Parents, pupils and grant maintained schools, *British Educational Research Journal*, Vol. 20, no. 2, pp. 209–26.

Power, S., Whitty, G. and Youdell, D. (1995) *No Place to Learn: Homelessness and Education*. London: Shelter.

Proudford, C. and Baker, R. (1995) Schools that make a difference: a sociological perspective on effective schooling, *British Journal of Sociology of Education*, Vol. 16, no. 3, pp. 277–92.

Pryke, R. (1996) Positioning the LEA in LEArning, *Education Journal*, Vol. 6, p. 21.

Putnam, R. D. (1993) The prosperous community: social capital and public life, *American Prospect*, Vol. 13, Spring.

Putnam, R. D., with Leonardi, R. and Nanetti, R. Y. (1993) *Making Democracy Work: Civic Traditions in Modern Italy*. Princeton, NJ: Princeton University Press.

Pyke, N. (1997) Billions fail to add up to rising standards, *Times Educational Supplement*, 3 October, p.1.

Ranson, S. (2000) Recognizing the pedagogy of voice in a learning community, *Educational Management and Administration*, Vol. 28, no. 3, pp. 263–79.

Raywid, M. A. (1994) *Focus Schools: A Genre to Consider*, Urban Diversity Series No. 106. New York: Columbia University, ERIC Clearinghouse on Urban Education.

Reay, D. and Ball, S. (1998) 'Making their minds up': family dynamics and school choice, *British Educational Research Journal*, Vol. 24, pp. 431–48.

Reynolds, D. (1997) Now we must tackle social inequality not just assess it, *Times Educational Supplement*, 21 March, p. 23.

Riddell, P. (1992) Is it the end of politics? *The Times*, 3 August.

Roberts, P. (1994) Business sponsorship in schools: a changing climate, in Bridges, D. and McLaughlin, T. (eds), *Education and the Market Place*. London: Falmer Press.

Robertson, S. L. (1993) The politics of devolution, self-management and post-Fordism in schools, in Smyth, J. (ed.), *A Socially Critical View of the Self-Managing School*. London: Falmer Press.

Robertson, S. L. (1995) *'Free' Capitalism and 'Fast' Schools*. Paper presented to the American Educational Association Annual Meeting, San Francisco, 18–22 April.

Robertson, S. L. (1996) *Markets and Teacher Professionalism*. Paper presented at the Ninth World Congress of Comparative Education Societies, Sydney, Australia, 1–6 July.

Robins, K. (1991) Tradition and translation: national culture in its global context, in Corner, J. and Harvey, S. (eds), *Enterprise and Heritage: Crosscurrents of National Culture*. London: Routledge.

Robinson, P. (1997) *Literacy, Numeracy and Economic Performance*. London:

CEP/London School of Economics.

Rose, L. C. and Gallup, A. M. (1999) The 31st Annual Phi Delta Kappa/ Gallup Poll, *Phi Delta Kappa*, Vol. 81, no. 1, pp. 41–56.

Rose, N. and Miller, P. (1992) Political power beyond the state: problematics of government, *British Journal of Sociology*, Vol. 43, no. 2, pp. 173–205.

Rossell, C. H. and Glenn, C. L. (1988) The Cambridge controlled choice plan, *Urban Review*, Vol. 20, no. 2, pp. 75–94.

Rowe, D. (1993) Citizenship, PSE and the French dressing approach to curriculum planning, *Social Science Teacher*, Vol. 22, no. 2, pp. 16–17.

Rutter, M., Maughan, B., Mortimore, P. and Ouston, J. (1979) *Fifteen Thousand Hours*. London: Open Books.

Schweinhart, L. J. and Weikart, D. P. (1997) Lasting differences: the High/ Scope pre-school curriculum comparison study through age 23, *Early Childhood Research Quarterly*, Vol. 12, no. 2, pp. 117–43.

Schweinhart, L. J., Barnes, H. V. and Weikart, D. P. (1993) Significant benefits: the High/Scope Perry preschool study through age 27, *Monographs of the High/Scope Educational Research Foundation*, Vol. 10.

Selwyn, N. (1999) Gilding the Grid: the marketing of the National Grid for Learning, *British Journal of Sociology*, Vol. 20, no. 1, pp. 55–68.

Sexton, S. (1987) *Our Schools – a Radical Policy*. Warlingham: IEA Education Unit.

Shilling, C. (1993) The demise of sociology of education in Britain? *British Journal of Sociology of Education*, Vol. 14, no. 1, pp. 105–12.

Shorrocks, D., Daniels, S., Frobisher, L., Nebon, N., Waterson, A. and Bell, S. (1992) *Enca 1 Project: The Evaluation of National Curriculum Assessment at Key Stage 1*. Leeds: School of Education, University of Leeds.

Simon, B. (1994) *The State and Educational Change*. London: Lawrence & Wishart.

Sinclair, J., Ironside, M. and Seifert, R. (1993) *Classroom Struggle? Market Oriented Education Reforms and Their Impact on Teachers' Professional Autonomy, Labour Intensification and Resistance*. Paper presented at the International Labour Process Conference, 1 April.

Smith, A. B. and Gaffney, M. (1997) *Evaluation of the TIE Project: A Preliminary Report*. Dunedin: Children's Issues Centre.

Smith, C. and Pugh, G. (1996) *Learning to Be a Parent: A Survey of Group-Based Parenting Programmes*. London: Family Policies Studies Centre.

Smith, G. (1987) Whatever happened to educational priority areas? *Oxford Review of Education*, Vol. 13, no. 1, pp. 23–38.

Smith, K. B. and Meier, K. J. (1995) *The Case Against School Choice: Politics, Markets and Fools*. Armonk, NY: M. E. Sharpe.

Smith, T. and Noble, M. (1995) *Education Divides: Poverty and Schooling in the 1990s*. London: Child Poverty Action Group.

Smithers, A. (2001) Labour creating secondary maze, *Guardian*, 24 May.

Socialist Teachers Alliance (1998) *Trojan Horses: Education Action Zones – the Case Against the Privatisation of Education*. London: Socialist Teachers Alliance.

Soucek, V. (1996) *Education Policy Formation in the Post-Fordist Era and Its Impact on the Nature of Teachers' Work*. Unpublished PhD thesis, University of Alberta.

Stepien, D., Murray, L. and Lawrence, B. (1996) *Homelessness, Schooling and Attainment*. Portsmouth: University of Portsmouth, Portsmouth City Council in association with LDJ Educational.

Stewart, W. A. C. (1967) *Karl Mannheim on Education and Social Thought*. London: George G. Harrap for the University of London, Institute of Education.

Stoll, L. and Fink, D. (1996) *Changing Our Schools*. Buckingham: Open University Press.

Stronge, J. H. (1992) The background: history and problems of schooling for the homeless, in Stronge, J. H. (ed.), *Educating Homeless Children and Adolescents: Evaluating Policy and Practice*. Newbury Park, CA: Sage Publications.

Sullivan, K. (1994) The impact of education reform on teachers' professional ideologies, *New Zealand Journal of Educational Studies*, Vol. 29, no. 1, pp. 3–20.

Sylva, K. and Wilshire, J. (1993) The impact of early learning on children's later development: a review prepared for the RSA Inquiry 'Start Right', *European Early Childhood Education Research Journal*, Vol. 1, no. 1, pp. 17–40.

Taylor, C. (2001) Specialist schools – the real facts behind their success, *Technology Colleges Trust News*, no. 18, Summer.

Taylor, W. (1996). Education and the Moot, in Aldrich, R. (ed.), *In History and in Education*. London: Woburn Press.

Thompson, K. (1992) Social pluralism and postmodernity in Hall, S., Held, D. and McGrew, T. (eds), *Modernity and Its Futures*. Cambridge: Polity Press.

Thrupp, M. (1995) The school mix effect: the history of an enduring problem in educational research, policy and practice, *British Journal of Sociology of Education*, Vol. 16, pp. 183–203.

Thrupp, M. (1999) *Schools Making a Difference: Let's be Realistic!* Buckingham: Open University Press.

Tooley, J. (1995) Markets or democracy? A reply to Stewart Ranson, *British Journal of Educational Studies*, Vol. 43, no. 1, pp. 21–34.

Tooley, J. (1996) *Education without the State*. London: Institute of Economic Affairs.

Tooley, J. (2000) *Reclaiming Education*. London: Cassell.

Tooley, J. and Darby, D. (1998) *Educational Research: A Critique*. London: OFSTED.

Torres, C. (1998) *Education, Power, and Personal Biography*. London: Routledge.

Townsend, P. (1996) Comment quoted in Richards, H., Perspectives, *Times Higher Education Supplement*, 30 August, p. 13.

Troman, G. (1996) The rise of the new professionals: the restructuring of primary teachers' work and professionalism, *British Journal of Sociology of Education*, Vol. 17, no. 4, pp. 473–87.

Tulloch, M. (2001) Promoting comprehensive education, in Chitty, C. and Simon, B. (eds), *Promoting Comprehensive Education in the 21st Century*. Stoke-on-Trent: Trentham Books.

Usher, R. and Edwards, R. (1994) *Postmodernism and Education*. London: Routledge.

Vincent, C., Evans, J., Lunt, I. and Young, P. (1995) Policy and practice: the changing nature of special educational provision in schools, *British Journal of Special Education*, Vol. 22, no. 1, pp. 4–11.

Wadsworth, M. E. J. (1996) Family and education as determinants of health, in Blane, D., Brunner, E. and Wilkinson, R. (eds), *Health and Social Organisation: Towards a Health Policy for the 21st Century*. London: Routledge.

Wadsworth, M. E. J. (1997a) Changing social factors and their long-term implications for health, *British Medical Bulletin*, Vol. 53, no. 1, pp. 198–209.

Wadsworth, M. E. J. (1997b) Health inequalities in the Life Course perspective, *Social Science and Medicine*, Vol. 44, no. 6, pp. 859–69.

Walford, G. (1992) Educational choice and equity in Great Britain, *Educational Policy*, Vol. 6, no. 2, pp. 123–38.

Walford, G. and Miller, H. (1991) *City Technology College*. Milton Keynes: Open University Press.

Walker, A. and Walker, C. (eds) (1997) *Britain Divided: the Growth of Social Exclusion in the 1980s and 1990s*. London: Child Poverty Action Group.

Waslander, S. and Thrupp, M. (1995) Choice, competition and segregation: an empirical analysis of a New Zealand secondary school market 1990–1993, *Journal of Education Policy*, Vol. 10, no. 1, pp. 1–26.

Weiss, M. (1993) New guiding principles in educational policy: the case of Germany, *Journal of Education Policy*, Vol. 8, no. 4, pp. 307–20.

Wells, A. S. (1993a) The sociology of school choice: why some win and others lose in the educational marketplace, in Rasell, E. and Rothstein, R. (eds), *School Choice: Examining the Evidence*. Washington, DC: Economic Policy Institute.

Wells, A. S. (1993b) *Time to Choose: America at the Crossroads of School Choice Policy*. New York: Hill & Wang.

Wells, A. S., Grutzik, C., Carnochan, S., Slayton, J. and Vasudeva, A. (1999) Underlying policy assumptions of Charter School reform: the multiple meanings of a movement, *Teachers College Record*, Vol. 100, no. 3, pp. 513–35.

West, A., Noden, P., Kleinman, M. and Whitehead, C. (2000) *Examining the Impact of the Specialist Schools Programme*. DfEE Research Report RR 196, Centre for Educational Research, London School of Economics and Political Science.

Wexler, P. (1992) *Becoming Somebody*. Lewes, Sussex: Falmer Press.

Whitty, G. (1985) *Sociology and School Knowledge: Curriculum Theory, Research and Politics*. London: Methuen.

Whitty, G. (1992a) Education, economy and national culture, in Bocock, R. and Thompson, K. (eds), *Social and Cultural Forms of Modernity*. Cambridge: Polity Press.

Whitty, G. (1992b) Integrated humanities and world studies, in Rattansi, A. and Reeder, D. (eds), *Radicalism and Education: Essays for Brian Simon*. London: Lawrence & Wishart.

Whitty, G. (1994) Devolution in education systems: implications for teacher professionalism and pupil performance, *National Industry Education Forum: Decentralisation and Teachers: Report of a Seminar*. Melbourne: National Industry Education Forum.

Whitty, G. (1997) Creating quasi-markets in education: a review of recent research on parental choice and school autonomy in three countries, *Review of Research in Education*, Vol. 22, pp. 3–47.

Whitty, G. and Edwards, T. (1998) School choice policies in Britain and the United States: an exploration of their origins and significance, *Comparative Education*, Vol. 34, no. 2, pp. 211–27.

Whitty, G. and Power, S. (1999) Making sense of education reform: global and national influences, *International Journal of Contemporary Sociology*, Vol. 36, no. 2, pp. 144–62.

Whitty, G. and Power, S. (2000) Marketization and privatization in mass education systems, *International Journal of Educational Development*, Vol. 20, pp. 93–107.

Whitty, G., Edwards, T. and Gewirtz, S. (1993) *Specialisation and Choice in Urban Education: The City Technology College Experiment*. London: Routledge.

Whitty, G., Power, S. and Edwards, T. (1998) The assisted places scheme: its impact and its role in privatization and marketization, *Journal of Education Policy*, Vol. 13, no. 2, pp. 237–50.

Whitty, G., Power, S. and Halpin, D. (1998) *Devolution and Choice in Education: The School, the State and the Market*. Buckingham: Open University Press.

Whitty, G., Rowe, G. and Aggleton, P. (1994a) Discourse in cross-curricular contexts: limits to empowerment, *International Studies in Sociology of Education*, Vol. 4, no. 1, pp. 25–42.

Whitty, G., Rowe, G. and Aggleton, P. (1994b) Subjects and themes in the secondary school curriculum, *Research Papers in Education*, Vol. 9, no. 2, pp. 159–81.

Whitty, G., Aggleton, P., Gamarnikow, E. and Tyrer, P. (1998) Education and health inequalities, *Journal of Education Policy*, Vol. 13, no. 5, pp. 641–52.

Wilby, P. (1998) Why not try old ideas? *Times Educational Supplement*, 13 February, p. 22.

Wilkinson, R. G. (1994) Health, redistribution and growth, in Glyn, A. and Miliband, D. (eds), *Paying for Inequality: The Economic Cost of Social Justice*. London: IPPR/Rivers Oram.

Wilkinson, R. G. (1996) *Unhealthy Societies: the Afflictions of Inequality*. London: Routledge.

Wilkinson, R. (1997) *Unfair Shares: the Effects of Widening Income Differences on the Welfare of the Young*. London: Barnardos.

Willms, J. D. (1999) Quality and inequality in children's literacy: the effects of families, schools and communities, in Keating, D. P. and Hertzman, C. (eds), *Developmental Health and the Wealth of Nations: Social, Biological and Educational Dynamics*. New York: Guilford, pp. 72–93.

Witte, J. F., Thorn, C. A., Pritchard, K. M. and Claibourn, M. (1994) *Fourth Year Report: Milwaukee Parental Choice Program*. Madison, WI, Department of Public Instruction.

Witte, J. F., Thorn, C. A. and Pritchard, K. (1995) *Private and Public Education in Wisconsin: Implications for the Choice Debate*. Madison, WI: University of Wisconsin.

Wohlstetter, P., Wenning, R. and Briggs, K. L. (1995) Charter Schools in the United States: the question of autonomy, *Educational Policy*, Vol. 9, no. 4, pp. 331–58.

Woldring, H. E. S. (1986) *Karl Mannheim: The Development of His Thought*. Assen/Maastricht: Van Gorcum.

Woodhead, C. (1998) Academia gone to seed, *New Statesman*, 20 March.

Woodroffe, C., Glickman, M., Barker, M. and Power, C. (1993) *Children, Teenagers and Health: The Key Data*. Buckingham: Open University Press.

Wright, E. O. (1995) The real utopias project, 'Preface' in Cohen, J. and Rogers, J. (eds), *Associations and Democracy*. London: Verso.

Wylie, C. (1994) *Self Managing Schools in New Zealand: the Fifth Year*. Wellington: New Zealand Council for Educational Research.

Wylie, C. (1995) Contrary currents: the application of the Public Sector Reform Framework in Education, *New Zealand Journal of Educational Studies*, Vol. 20, no. 2, pp. 149–64.

Wylie, C. (1997) *Self Managing Schools Seven Years On – What Have We Learnt?* Wellington: New Zealand Council for Educational Research.

Wylie, C. (1998a) *School Self-Management in New Zealand: How Can It Make a Difference?* Address to NZCER Annual Conference, 21 October.

Wylie, C (1998b) *Can Vouchers Deliver Better Education? A Review of the Literature with Special Reference to New Zealand*. Wellington: New Zealand Council for Educational Research.

Wylie, C. (1999a) Is the land of the flightless bird now the home of the voucherless voucher? *New Zealand Journal of Educational Research*, Vol. 34, no. 1, pp. 99–109.

Wylie, C. (1999b) *Choice, Responsiveness and Constraint after a Decade of Self-Managing Schools in New Zealand*. Paper delivered at AARE-NZARE conference, Melbourne, Australia.

Young, M. F. D. (ed.) (1971) *Knowledge and Control: New Directions for the Sociology of Education*. London: Collier Macmillan.

Young, M. F. D. (1973) Taking sides against the probable, *Educational Review*, Vol. 25, no. 3, pp. 210–22.

Young, M. (1998a) 'Right questions, wrong answers', Letter to the *New Statesman*, 3 April.

Young, M. (1998b) *The Curriculum of the Future*. London: Falmer Press.

Young, M. (1999) Some reflections on the concepts of social exclusion and inclusion: beyond the third way, in Hayton, A. (ed.), *Tackling Disaffection and Social Exclusion*. London: Kogan Page.

Young, M. and Whitty, G. (eds) (1977) *Society, State and Schooling: Readings on the Possibilities for Radical Education*. Lewes: Falmer Press.

Zeichner, K. and Liston, D. (1987) Teaching student teachers how to reflect, *Harvard Educational Review*, Vol. 57, pp. 23–48.

Index